49 ½

SKIRTS

49 ½

SKIRTS

Alison Willoughby

A QUARTO BOOK

First published in 2008 by
A&C Black Publishers
38 Soho Square
London W1D 3HB
www.acblack.com

Copyright © 2008 Quarto Publishing plc

ISBN 978 0 7136 8740 8

A CIP record for this book is available
from the British Library.

Conceived, designed and produced by
Quarto Publishing plc
The Old Brewery
6 Blundell Street
London N7 9BH

QUA: FFSK

Project editor: Katy Bevan
Assistant editor: Emma Poulter
Managing art editor: Anna Plucinska
Designer: Jackie Palmer
Photographer: Andrew Atkinson
Stylist: Lone Sigurdsson
Art director: Caroline Guest

Creative director: Moira Clinch
Publisher: Paul Carslake

Color separation by Modern Age Repro
House Ltd, Hong Kong

Printed by Midas Printing International
Ltd, China

To My Dearest Mum,
I wouldn't have been able
to do this 'skirt thang'
without you.

Thank you for all
your support.

A.W.

CONTENTS

FOREWORD

I make skirts, elaborate and lightweight skirts, that are sold and exhibited internationally.

Why skirts? As a textile designer my medium is fabric, and the flat surface of the skirt is an ideal canvas to apply multi-layered and manipulated fabric, as well as paint, printing ink, plastic, thread, wool, metal, glass and other materials – either from traditional dressmaking or those used in industrial manufacture.

The inspiration for the colour, texture and pattern I use comes mostly from photographs. The inspiration for the three-dimensional aspect of my work is recorded by photography, and comes from urban and domestic surfaces: accidental textures, evolving and weathered walls, marks and stains and kaleidoscopes of colour. All these images are transferred into fabrics and finally onto the skirt.

The first section of this book includes information on how to select and combine fabrics, colour, texture and pattern. This involves that tricky thing – personal taste. You'll also learn about deconstruction, construction stitches, decorative stitches, using paper patterns, basic seams, making a lining, closures and finishing. The remainder of the book provides step-by-step instructions to make a wide range of skirts, using a number of techniques, fabrics and finishings. Sources of inspiration for each design are disclosed: We are not practising traditional dressmaking here, this is 'skirtmaking', and it's very different.

SKIRTMAKING

INSPIRATION

Choosing a source for your inspiration is very subjective. Whatever you choose, it has to be something that you love, not a secondary image – for example an image out of a magazine or someone else's work – but something that is your own work. You need to make it your own – it should be your image, your photograph, your video or your drawing. If the image is your own first-hand inspiration, then you will have a strong base – something to look back to and rely upon later in the design process.

If you are stuck for inspiration, try this technique: enlarge a favourite image or photograph. Increasing an image's dimensions not only creates a larger area to look at, but the details that were tiny become larger and more abstracted. Take the photo and put it on a large piece of paper so there is space to look at it, with nothing else distracting the eye. First, look at the whole image and do a colour study of it: mix paint to match the photographs. Secondly, use a viewfinder (a piece of paper with a rectangle or square cut into the middle of it) to do a colour study of a favourite area in the photograph. Examine the exact colours again – how many different reds are there in the world? Tomato red, fire engine red, rust red, apple red, radish red, terracotta red, traffic-light red, rouge red... By focusing in on a smaller area, you will find it easier to mix the colours you need.

Shape and texture can be explored in much the same way. Looking at the minute details is crucial for this way of working. Study the detail, make a drawing of it, change the scale of it and make a sketch from it, or on it. These marks can be transferred, quite literally, straight onto a textile, whether this is by drawing and painting straight onto the fabric, or screen printing and embroidering straight onto fabric. Texture can be represented by a certain quality of fabric – for example, PVC is good to represent a shiny painted surface, and mohair is good to represent a fluffy cloud, or a dog's hairy coat.

CHOOSING FABRIC

The type of material that you choose for your skirts will be integral to the final result and its success, or otherwise. Thick, heavyweight fabrics, like cotton twill or denim, will be tough and wear well. However, too many layers of weighty material will be challenging to wear. Conversely, expecting lightweight silky fabrics to support a complicated ruffle or embellishments would be foolhardy. Balance a sturdy layer, with a finer lining, or match your ambitions to the fabric you have in hand.

1 There are plenty of decorative fabrics available. Most shops will allow you to buy small amounts, or to take swatches away with you.

2 An artist's studio is a fascinating place. A repository for found objects, inspirational photographs, sketches and swatches, as well as current work in progress.

3 Fabrics can be found in all sorts of places, as well as traditional dressmaking sources. Markets can often provide unexpected finds, and Indian sari shops have beautifully coloured lightweight silks.

4 Stores that cater to particular disciplines may yield great finds. This particular shop is in London's Soho, and supplies theatrical costumiers as well as the local burlesque shows.

5 Charity shops and antique markets are a treasure trove of inspirational finds, from costume jewellery to artificial fruits.

6 Work that is nearing completion can be hung in your work space while you decide what finishing touches it may require.

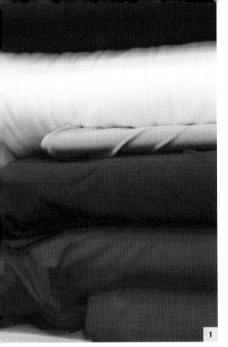
1

2

3

4

5

6

DECONSTRUCTION

Deconstruction makes use of the old and is one method of creating something new and innovative. This can be quite traumatic for some people, but your great-granny's dresses will only sit in a drawer, under a bed or in the attic, and get moth-eaten or mouldy if you let them. By deconstructing, or taking garments apart, you are putting the pieces back together again in a different form, or adding them to another garment. By revealing their construction, you are recycling and manipulating old and rejected garments and making them new again.

Objects can be collected and recovered from granny's attic, second-hand and antique shops, yard sales and charity shops and incorporated into your work. These vintage items have been witness to past lives. They have a history and character that it would be difficult to re-create.

1 Old skirts are often not good enough to wear any more, but the fabric may be of good quality and has plenty of life left in it. Cut it up and start again, or use parts of the skirts as additions as they are.

2 A well-fitting skirt can be updated by using it as the base for your embellishments, and saves the work of making the whole skirt from scratch.

3 Tapestries and embroidery, especially elaborately decorated linens are ideal for cutting up and using again. Any broken, or soiled parts can be cut away, and the image distorted, so all that remains is the colour and texture.

4 In order to make new, you have to do some cutting. Don't be timid – have the courage of your convictions, and cut with impunity.

5 Don't limit yourself to just skirts. Old ties and scarves are ideal for recycling. First, unpick any seams and remove any stitching.

6 Press the deconstructed items flat with a warm iron, being careful to use a temperature that is appropriate for the fabric. If you are not sure, use a damp cloth to protect the fabric and the iron from damage.

EQUIPMENT
You will need a variety of sharp blades for deconstructing.

1 A pair of snipper-type small scissors are good for loose ends.

2 General scissors can be used for cutting paper and anything else.

3 Dressmaking shears should be kept for fabric only, or they will blunt.

4 Use a self-healing cutting mat with a craft knife or scalpel.

5 A seam ripper or quick unpick is an inexpensive, but priceless tool.

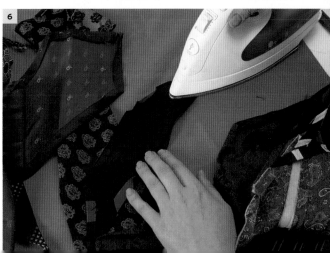

CONSTRUCTION

As with any kind of construction, you need the right tools for the job. It is possible to manage without a sewing machine, but having one makes sewing easier and quicker. There are also a few other items that will make the path of creation smoother.

TAILOR'S CHALK
Chalk is a traditional material for marking cloth and can be brushed away when finished with. Keep the edges sharp and use a colour that shows up well on the fabric. Powdered chalk is available with a roller for precise marking.

SEWING NEEDLES
There are many different hand needles available to suit the task, the cloth and the thread being used. Sharps are small, medium-length needles with small eyes for general sewing. Embroidery needles have larger holes to take embroidery floss. Special beading needles are long and extra-fine to pass through the holes in beads.

TAPE MEASURE
Choose a good quality tape that doesn't stretch. A yardstick, or smaller ruler will also be useful.

THREADS
Sewing threads come in several weights and compositions, and myriad colours. Polyester and 100% cotton threads are suitable for most general sewing. Thicker threads are available for topstitching that will be on display, while button thread can be used for extra strength and security.

MACHINE NEEDLES
These are available to suit most kinds of fabric. Standard needles are used for general stitching, while specialist needles are used for jersey, microfibre or leather. Heavyweight jeans needles will penetrate heavy cloth, or many layers of fabric, while finer needles are best for silk fabrics.

PINS
Using the correct pins and needles can save hours of frustration. Dressmaking pins are finer than household pins. Silk pins are finer still, and won't damage delicate fabrics.

SEWING MACHINE NEEDLES
Needle size is denoted by numbers: the larger the number, the larger the needle. American sizes are followed by the European system: Choose a $^8/_{60}$ needle for lightweight fabrics; a $^{10}/_{70}$ or $^{12}/_{80}$ needle for medium-weights; a $^{14}/_{90}$ or $^{16}/_{100}$ for heavy fabrics like jeans or canvas, and $^{18}/_{110}$ or $^{19}/_{120}$ for very heavyweight fabrics.

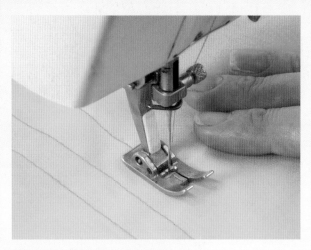

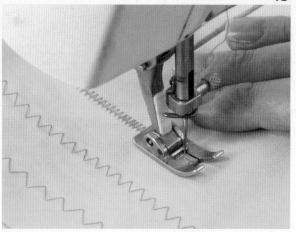

STRAIGHT STITCH

A straight stitch is the original and most useful machine stitch. It is very versatile and will allow most techniques to be undertaken, including seams, pleating and ruching. Adjust the length of the stitch according to the weight of fabric – the finer the fabric, the shorter the stitch.

ZIGZAG STITCH

The length and width of a zigzag stitch can be adjusted to suit different projects. Set the machine to its full width and then adjust the length to gain the effect you need – close together for embroidery, or wider for stitching stretch fabrics. Use to neaten fraying edges, for appliqué and for mending.

SECURING THREADS

When you reach the end of your row or seam, it is important to fasten the ends so the stitches don't unravel. As with most things, there is the quick way, backtacking, and the slow way, stitching by hand, that looks neater for when the seam end will be on show.

BACKTACKING

The easy way to stop the ends of your seams unravelling, especially where it won't show, is to stitch backwards and forwards along the seam line. To do this, sew to the end of the seam, put the machine into reverse – most machines have an easily accessible lever – and sew for a short distance back, and forth again.

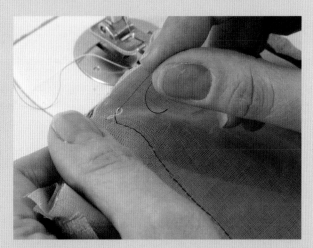

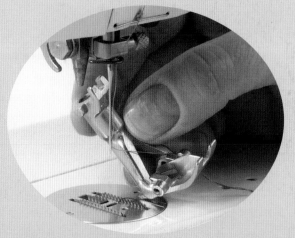

TYING ENDS

Pull the thread on the wrong side, so that the thread from underneath comes through. Tie the ends together in a square knot, and use a needle to sew back along the line of stitching before cutting off the ends.

CHANGING A FOOT

To change the foot on your machine, release the foot lever, being careful not to break the needle.

EMBELLISHMENT

Fabrics and threads lend themselves to a decorative approach –
buttons, embroidery floss, fabric inks and assorted ribbons are
the paints of the textile artist. All manner of items can be used to
embellish fabric – collections and stashes may overtake your
living space once you get the collecting bug.

1 BUTTON BADGES
Industrial quantities of any
single item can create an impact:
These badges will make an
armour-like finish to a skirt.

2 OTHER MATERIALS
Zips have a well-known
use, but they can also be used
decoratively. Take a sideways
look at any materials that come
your way: keys, beads, artificial
flowers or small plastic toys can
all be used as decorations.

3 BUTTONS
An old biscuit tin of buttons is
a treasure chest for a creative
person, offering material to work
with, as well as inspiration. Snap
up any old buttons, closures and
beads that you find to build up
your stash.

4 RIBBON AND TAPE
All sorts of ribbon, tape and cord
are useful for decorating. Once
you start to collect, you will be
saving ribbons from all sorts of
places – gift wrappings, smart
store-bag handles, clothing tags
– and hoarding.

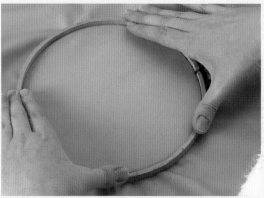

HOOPS

Embroidery hoops are useful for both hand and machine sewing as they hold the fabric flat and prevent stitches distorting the fabric as you sew. Choose a hoop of an appropriate size – a small hoop can be moved around as you work. Make sure they are kept clean, so as not to mark the surface of the fabric. If the wood becomes damaged, bind the hoop with tape to prolong its life and protect your work.

USING AN EMBROIDERY HOOP

1 Place the smaller part of the hoop underneath the fabric so there is a good amount of spare fabric on each side.

2 Put the larger circle over the top, and push down evenly to stretch the fabric.

GLUE GUN

A hot glue gun may not seem like a necessary item, but once you have used one, you'll wonder what you did without it. The glue comes in rods that are replaceable. They are messy, so keep a spare cloth handy.

3 Tighten the screw fitting to hold the fabric firmly while you are working on that area.

PAPER PATTERNS

In the envelope at the back of this book, there is a large sheet of paper with the pattern for a skirt and other templates for you to use. You may wish to use these designs more than once, so it is a good idea to transfer the images onto tracing paper, newsprint or other large sheets of paper, with a fibre-tip or marker pen.

COPYING THE PATTERN
Lay the pattern sheet out on a large table or on the floor. Place your blank paper over the top, and copy all the markings. Write the name of each piece on the new copy to remind you what they are.

ADJUSTING THE SIZE
When you need to adjust the size of a skirt, measure the skirt first. Then measure the person it is to be made for and make any alterations. Use the lengthening and shortening line to extend or crop the length of the skirt. Be sure to allow extra width if necessary. Since the skirt here is a wrap skirt, the width can be added at the side – if it is too large, the skirt will just wrap further around. Ties and closures can be strategically positioned to fit (see pages 22-25). Cut out this tailored pattern and mark it with the recipient's name for further use. You will need it again to cut out the lining.

YOU WILL NEED
- → fabric cutting shears
- → paper scissors
- → tracing paper
- → fibre-tip pen
- → dressmaking pins

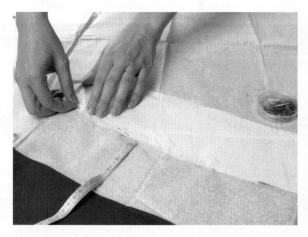

TO LENGTHEN
If the pattern is not long enough, adjust it to the correct size by adding an extra piece of paper at the bottom, and pin the papers together.

TO SHORTEN
If the pattern is too long for your measurements, mark the correct measurement on your paper pattern an equal length all along the bottom, then cut off.

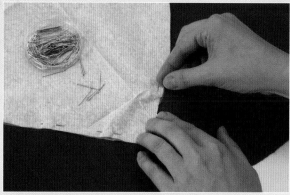

MARKING AND CUTTING

1 Lay the fabric on a flat surface. If you don't have a large enough table, use a clean floor. Fold the fabric in half, making sure the selvedges (see below) are level. Place your pattern on the double layer of fabric, making sure it takes up the least amount of room possible, so you get the most from your materials.

2 Flatten the paper on the fabric and pin into place around the edges. The straight line at the centre of the skirt should follow the straight of the grain. If you are cutting two pieces, add a 1 cm (3/8 in) seam allowance at the edge. Otherwise, place the centreline on the fold of the fabric, and then a seam won't be needed. Whether you can do this will depend on the width of the cloth being used.

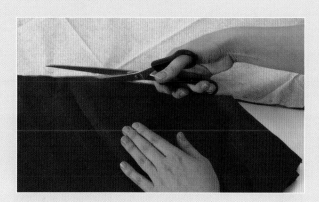

3 Using shears kept especially for cutting cloth, cut out the fabric following the edge of your pattern.

4 Once all the pieces are cut out, remove the pins, and keep the paper pattern carefully folded up.

PATTERN SYMBOLS

⟷ Straight grain
Place this line parallel to the selvedge

↰↑ Fold line
Place the arrows on the folded edge

– – – – – – – – – – – –
Seam allowance
Allow 1 cm (3/8 in) for the seam

– – – – – – – – – – – –
Join line
This is where you join the paper pattern pieces

SELVEDGES
These are literally the finished edges of a woven cloth that do not unravel. The selvedge will usually be the straightest edge to help line up your straight pattern pieces and find the line of the grain, or the lines of the warp (the first threads on the loom before a fabric is woven) and weft (the threads woven between the warp threads to create a woven cloth).

FABRIC QUANTITIES
You will need about 2 m (2 yd) of fabric for the top layer of each skirt. You may have to adjust this according to the width of the fabric, and if you need to lengthen or shorten your pattern. For ribbon, or other materials, you can work with what you have collected, and stop when it is used up.

MAKING

Now that you have your fabric cut out you can move on to the next stage. If your skirt is in two halves, sew it together at this stage. The lining can also be added now, or you may prefer to add extra layers after you have completed the decoration. Adding the lining will also complete the waistline edge of the skirt.

SEAMS

A plain seam is the easiest and most versatile method of joining two pieces of fabric together.

1 With right sides together, pin along the sewing line.

THE SKIRT SEAM

1 If your skirt is in two halves, you will need to sew them together. Place the right sides of fabric together, match up the straight edges and pin.

2 Baste along the sewing line 1–1.5 cm ($^3/_8$–$^5/_8$ in) from the edge, or whatever seam allowance is specified in the pattern. Remove the pins.

2 Sew a plain seam 1 cm ($^3/_8$ in) from the edge, removing the pins as you go.

3 Set the sewing machine to a medium-length straight stitch and sew along the line. Tie ends and press open.

MAKING A LINING

The lining of a skirt is a mirror of the skirt itself, and serves several purposes: it will help the skirt to drape well when it's worn, fill out the silhouette and also make it warmer. Traditionally, lining fabric is a fine silky cloth, although you can use any cloth you like, as long as it will be comfortable next to your skin.

Cut another piece of fabric with the same pattern piece you used for the main skirt. You can cut as many linings as you like, and stitch them all together. Plenty of layers to a skirt will give it extra dramatic impact, but keep in mind that it will also add weight.

Above: Every skirt needs a lining, but it doesn't have to hide away, it can show through where the skirt flaps open – it can even be made into a feature.

TIP
The lining is usually the last thing to be added to your skirt, after all the embellishments. Any untidiness at the waist edge can be taken into the lining seam and hidden.

1 Pin the same paper pattern to the lining fabric you have chosen, and pin as before.

2 Cut out the lining fabric carefully.

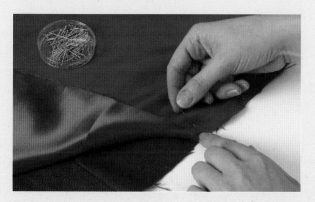

3 Pin the lining and skirt pieces right sides together, along the waistline edge.

4 Sew the lining and skirt together, leaving a 1 cm ($^3/_8$ in) seam allowance. Turn the lining to the inside, and press the edge by rolling the seam between finger and thumb. Secure the seam further by topstitching 2 mm ($^1/_{16}$ in) from the folded edge.

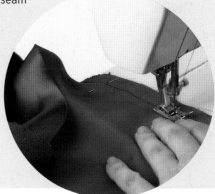

CLOSURES

Closures can become a feature, as well as being practical. There are a number of closures available to you, although depending on the fabric used and the style of your garment, some may be more suitable than others.

Above: This skirt uses a combination of ties and metal clasps to hold it together. This style of closure threads the ties through and grips them to close.

CLIPS
This kind of clip is strong enough to hold a skirt together and easy to attach. Some clips allow for fabric ties to pass through (see left), and some use a metal loop. Bar and hook closures for skirts are also suitable.

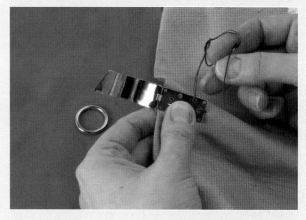

1 Open out the clip, and attach it to the outside flap of the skirt with strong sewing thread.

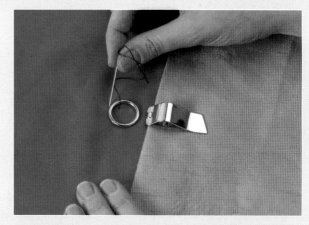

2 Sew the loop to the underside of the opening with several strong stitches.

SNAP CLOSURES

Snaps can be tiny, or quite large, but the method to sew them on is the same. They can be a useful addition to ties if your skirt is prone to flap open. If they are to be used on their own, they will need to be large, and you will need to use more than one, to take the weight of a skirt with linings.

Use a needle and strong – or double thickness – sewing thread.

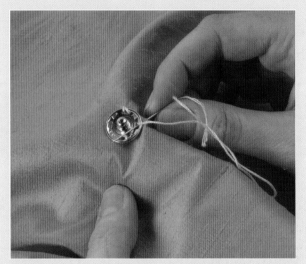

1 Stitch the first half in position using several hand stitches at each corner.

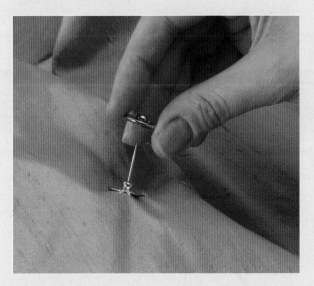

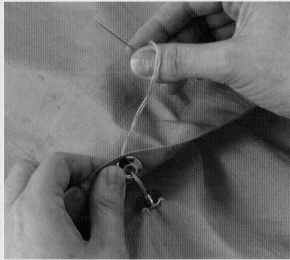

2 Break the thread. Push the needle up through the central hole of the press stud in order to achieve the correct alignment.

3 Sew directly through the second half, into the next part of the fabric and secure in place at the sides, removing the central thread.

TIES

As the main closures for the skirt are at the waistline, you can make ties in the same fabric as the main skirt, or the lining, or in a contrasting fabric. Use the tie templates on the pattern sheet provided. Use your ties with metal clips, or sew one to each side of the skirt and tie in a bow or simple knot.

1 Remove the pins from the two tie pieces and save the pattern piece for further use.

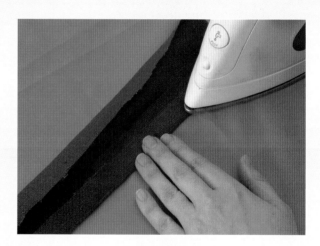

2 Fold the long edges in by 1 cm ($^3/_8$ in) and press. Fold both pieces in half lengthways, and press again.

Left: Make your ties as long as you like, and use as many as you want, to create a striking feature.

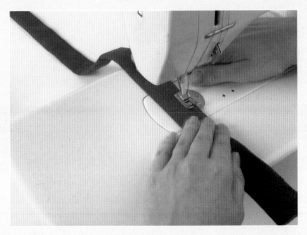

3 Set the machine to a straight stitch, and topstitch along the edge to hold it together.

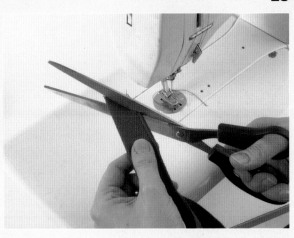

4 Cut one end of each tie diagonally to finish.

5 Position the ties on either side of the waistline. The best way to do this is to try the skirt on, find the correct position and pin. Using a machine straight stitch, make a square at the straight end to attach the ties to the skirt.

6 Reinforce this by stitching diagonally across the square for extra strength.

GOING ROUND CORNERS
When you need to turn a corner, wait until the needle is in the fabric at the corner point, raise the foot and spin the fabric around, and then lower the foot and continue stitching in the new direction.

FINISHING

The hem of the skirt doesn't have to involve complicated sewing, and leaving the edge unfinished doesn't mean that your skirt will unravel as you wear it. You may decide to make a hem, but otherwise a frayed edge can look great.

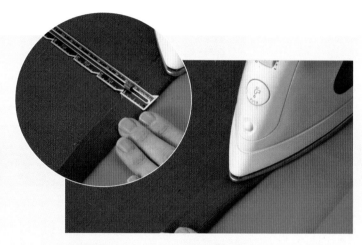

FRAYED EDGES
Trim the skirt to your preferred length. Use a needle to pull more threads at the frayed edge away, and then trim to the same length to neaten. The fabric then frays at its own pace.

MAKING A HEM
1 If you prefer to make a proper hemline, measure 2.5 cm (1 in) and fold the raw edge under to the wrong side. Press with a hot iron. Fold over the edge again, pressing the fabric flat.

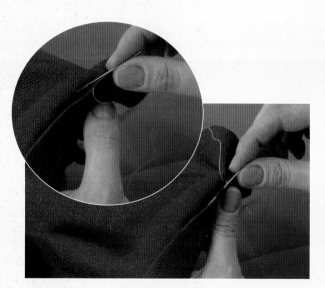

2 To work a slip stitch along this edge, work from right to left, and pick up a single thread of the main fabric with the needle. Insert the needle into the fold of the fabric, pull through and repeat.

3 Pull the stitches firmly, without puckering. If you use a thread the same colour as the fabric, the stitches should be almost invisible on the right side.

Below: As the skirt hooks will remain hidden during wear, any colour or type of fabric can be used. Make use of any surplus material.

Above: Skirt hooks will allow your skirts to hang unencumbered while in storage.

TIP

Since there will be so many different materials in your skirts, it is recommended that you only dry-clean them. If you have used sand or plastics it is best not to clean them at all.

SKIRT HOOKS

In order to hang your skirt easily when in storage, you will need to make some skirt hooks. These can be a simple length of tape, ribbon, or a piece of the fabric used for the main skirt that has been strengthened, as below.

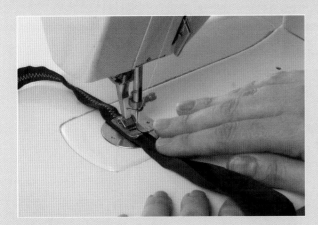

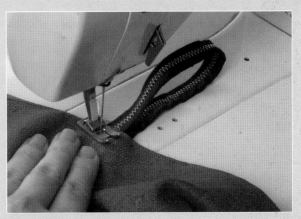

1 Cut a piece of fabric about 36 cm (14 in) long and 2.5 cm (1 in) wide. Fold the piece in three along its length and use a zigzag stitch to strengthen it.

2 Cut the long piece into two shorter pieces, and pin to the inside of the skirt at either side of the waist. Sew onto the lining, and then again at the top-stitched edge to secure.

THE COLLECTION

LOOPS & TAGS

A loop is simply a strip of fabric folded in half: that's it. A tag is similar, but shorter. More often, braiding or ribbon is used for shorter tags. Both loops and tags can be used to decorate and add texture to your skirt.

MAKING STRIPS

Following the straight of the grain, rip or cut strips of fabric to the width indicated in your pattern – about 2.5 cm (1 in) – and as long as the fabric allows. Some fabrics will be more suitable for tearing than others. Any fabric with a plain weave, that is where the warp and weft are regular, should be easy. Difficulties may occur when more complicated weaves are apparent, as in this yellow waffle-weave fabric. If you can't tear it, cut it.

Once you have a pile of strips, remove any excess threads and iron the strips so they are perfectly flat.

MAKING LOOPS

1 Measure about 8 cm (3½ in) from the bottom edge of the skirt, and mark a guideline with tailor's chalk.

2 Cut the strips into 15 cm (6 in) lengths. Fold each strip in half and align the edges with the chalk line. Pin the loops along the line, alternating colours, and overlapping the strips.

3 Using a machine, or by hand, sew along the edge to secure the loops. Line the next row of loops up, to conceal this row of stitching.

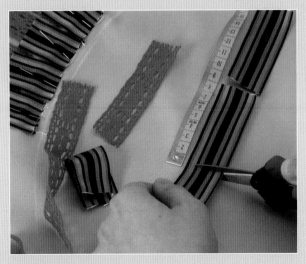

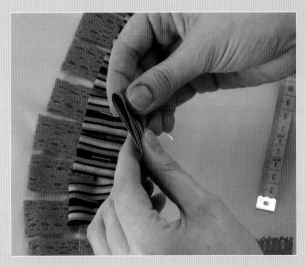

MAKING TAGS

1 Select your ribbon, Petersham tape or braid, and cut into approximately 8 cm (3½ in) lengths.

2 Fold the tags in half and press the fold with your fingers.

3 Measure about 8 cm (3½ in) from the bottom edge of the skirt, and mark a guideline with tailor's chalk. Pin the tags so that the raw edges are on the chalk guideline.

4 Sew along the edge of the line in order to secure the tags. Remove pins. Using tailor's chalk, mark another line 3.5 cm (1½ in) from this edge, and pin the next row of tags to this guideline.

SEWING FABRIC INTO SEAMS

Making extra seams in a skirt will reduce its width:
2 cm (³⁄₄ in) will be lost for each seam made. If you are
using a ready-made skirt take care to ensure that it still
fits (remember this when making a lining, as well).

1 Lay the skirt on a flat surface. Find the centreline, and
make a mark 10-12 cm (4-5 in) to one side at the top and
bottom edges, with the tailor's chalk. Using a measuring
tape or yardstick as a guide, draw a line vertically down
the centre of the skirt. Cut the skirt in half along the line.

2 Make strips of fabric as before, about 2 cm (³⁄₄ in)
wide and 56 cm (22 in) long. Iron them flat. Starting at
the waistband, take a strip, fold it in half and pin so that
the raw ends are flush with the edge of the skirt fabric.
Add another loop of fabric so it overlaps the first loop.
Continue until you reach the hem or run out of strips.

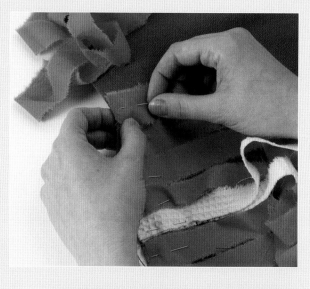

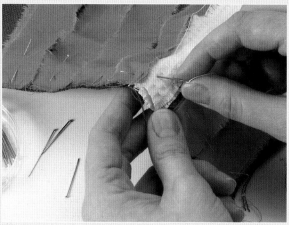

3 Baste the strips in place and remove the pins once
you have done so.

4 Place the other half of the skirt back on top, right
sides facing each other. Pin the two pieces together.

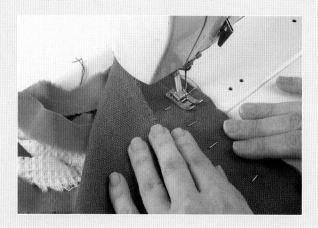

5 Sew with a 1 cm (³⁄₈ in) seam allowance, including all
loops into the seam. Backtack to secure, and then iron
both the seam and loops flat. Trim one side of the seam
allowance if it is bulky.

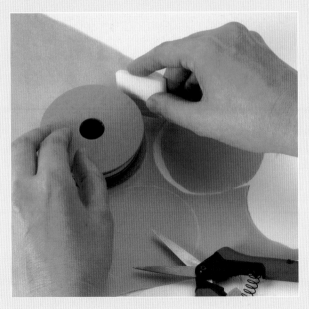

MAKING A SUFFOLK PUFF

1 Using tailor's chalk and a scrap of fabric, draw around a circular object about 7.5 cm (3 in) in diameter.

2 Cut out the circles following the chalk lines.

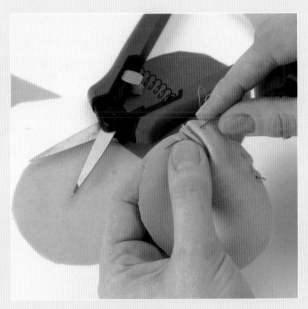

3 Making a simple knot in the end of some sewing thread, make a running stitch around the edge of each circle and gather tight.

4 Make a few stitches in the gathered circle to keep the puff closed. Continue until you have enough puffs for your project.

LOOP

1

MATERIALS & EQUIPMENT

→ **Second-hand skirt, or about 2 m (2 yd) fabric for skirt base – use the pattern sheet provided**

→ Corduroy fabric

SEE ALSO
Making, pages 20-21
Making loops, page 30

Sometimes great materials are limited and you have to work with what you have. This skirt is the result of having too much of one kind of fabric.

1. Cut out and make your skirt (see pages 8-27), or reclaim a skirt from a charity shop.

2. Rip the corduroy into uniform strips 2 cm (³/₄ in) wide and 20 cm (8 in) long.

3. Using tailor's chalk, draw a line 2 cm (³/₄ in) above the hemline all the way around the bottom of the skirt.

4. Take a strip of fabric and with the corduroy facing outwards, fold it in half to make a loop. Sew this to your line and repeat until the whole line is full.

5. Draw another line 2 cm (³/₄ in) up from your original line, towards the waistband, following around the skirt again. Repeat steps 4 and 5, until the whole skirt is full.

6. When you reach the top edge of the skirt, allow the raw edges of the loops to line up with the edge of the fabric. These edges will be taken into the seam when the lining is attached (see Making a lining, page 21).

PLUME

2

MATERIALS & EQUIPMENT

→ **Second-hand skirt, or about 2 m (2 yd) fabric for skirt base – use the pattern sheet provided**
→ Contrasting fabric for loops
→ Dressmaking pins

SEE ALSO

Making loops, page 30
Sewing fabric into seams, page 32

TIP

The selvedge (neat edge) of woven fabrics is often a different colour, or has type on it or some textural interest, so cut some strips from here for the loops.

Inspired by a drawer full of fabrics, threads, yarn and ribbons too thick or too awkward to sew, this skirt uses almost any fabric to create a surface that is textured but wearable. Leave the hem raw to complete the effect.

1. Cut out and make your skirt (see pages 8-27), or reclaim a skirt from a charity shop.

2. Take the fabric for your loops and tear into 30 strips, 56 cm (22 in) long, 2 cm (³/₄ in) wide. Remove any excess threads from the strips and iron flat.

3. Lay the skirt on a flat surface and find the centreline, then make a mark 10-12 cm (4-5 in) to one side with the tailor's chalk at the top and bottom edges. Using a measuring tape or yard stick as a guide, draw a line vertically down the centre of the skirt, cut the skirt in half then fold the skirt so the right sides are facing.

4. Starting at the waistband of the skirt, take a strip of fabric and fold it in half. Insert the fabric into the seam with the two loose ends on the seam line and pin. Add another loop of fabric so that it overlaps the first loop, continuing until you reach the hem (see page 32).

5. Sew the two pieces of skirt together with a 1 cm (³/₈ in) seam allowance, including all loops into the seam. Backtack to secure the seam. Press the seam and loops flat.

6. Hold the skirt up to you. Make a mark with the tailor's chalk to the right on the waistband, approximately 2 cm (³/₄ in) away from the first seam, doing the same at the hem edge. Using a ruler, draw a line with tailor's chalk that joins the two marks together. Repeat steps 3 and 4, being careful not to catch the previous loops in the seam – they should be flat and facing away from the sewing machine. Repeat again and you will end up with three strips of loops.

Cut the skirt like this

RED, WHITE & BLUE

MATERIALS & EQUIPMENT

→ **Second-hand skirt, or about 2 m (2 yd) fabric for skirt base (use a heavy fabric to support the weight of the ruffle) – use the pattern sheet provided**

→ Circle template A from pattern sheet

→ Heavy paper for template

→ Ribbon, Petersham tape and braiding

→ Brooches, buttons and beads

SEE ALSO
Making tags, page 31

TIP
Petersham is a tough stiffening tape traditionally used to make waistbands and wrap wires in corsetry. It looks similar to grosgrain ribbon but is identified by its uneven edge that enables it to stretch easily.

Five years of collecting ribbon and braid from charity shops, antique markets and Granny's attic inspired this skirt. Make a colour scheme that fits with your stash, so that you can recycle all those bits and pieces you have been hoarding.

1. Cut out and make your skirt (see pages 8–27), or reclaim a skirt from a charity shop that is patterned or plain.

2. Make a circle template with a diameter measuring 10 cm (4 in) less than the length of the skirt. Lay the skirt on a flat surface and mark the centreline. Place the circle template on the skirt so that it is 5 cm (2 in) from the top and bottom edges and to one side of the central line. Use tailor's chalk to draw around it.

3. Cut your ribbon, Petersham tape and braiding to 8 cm (3 1/8 in) lengths. Fold these in half and sew them to the chalk line, continuing all the way around until the circle is complete.

4. Measure 1 cm (3/8 in) away from the raw edges of the ribbon circle, and start the next circle of ribbon. Repeat until you have a circle of 30 cm (12 in) in diameter in the middle. Fill the circle with brooches, buttons and beads.

FISHERMAN

4

SEE ALSO
Making strips, page 30
Making tags, page 31
Making a stencil and using a silkscreen, page 83

A keen fisherman, my Grandpa fished on the Glenelly River, Ireland. His garage was full of different types of fishing paraphernalia and a large selection of nets, and I borrowed one net for this particular skirt. The fabric was originally bright tangerine orange, and I have printed onto the skirt, through the net, with a navy printing ink.

1. Cut out and make your skirt (see pages 8–27), or reclaim a skirt from a charity shop.

2. Lay the net on the skirt, as your stencil, and using navy ink, print all over with a blank screen. Let it dry.

3. Cut out your flower paper stencil and print through it with a white ink, so it sits on top of the already printed navy net.

4. Once the print is dry, remove the netting and iron the skirt on the reverse to fix the ink. Lay the skirt on a flat surface and mark the centreline. Place the circle template on the skirt so that it is 5 cm (2 in) from the bottom edge and to one side of the central line. Use tailor's chalk to draw around it.

5. Measure 6 cm (2¼ in) lengths of the cotton tape. Take a strip and fold it in half. Sew this to the chalk circle line and repeat until the whole circle joins up. Using the same process, fill the circle until there is roughly a 5 cm (2 in) area for your brooches, buttons and beads.

Note* Make sure the foot and needle of your sewing machine are on the left-hand side of the loop, while you are sewing in an anti-clockwise direction.

TEST MATCH

5

MATERIALS & EQUIPMENT

→ **Second-hand skirt, or about 2 m (2 yd) fabric for skirt base – use the pattern sheet provided**

→ Oval template D from pattern sheet

→ Heavy paper for template

→ Cotton tape, ribbon and Petersham tape

SEE ALSO
Making tags, page 31

These fresh greens are reminiscent of cricket lawns, and perhaps the shape echoes the famous Oval cricket ground in London, but there the analogy ends.

1. Cut out and make your skirt (see pages 8–27), or reclaim a skirt from a charity shop.

2. Make an oval template that is approximately 60 cm (24 in) long and 30 cm (12 in) wide.

3. Lay the skirt on a flat surface and draw a large oval on the skirt, at an angle.

4. Measure lengths of the cotton tape about 6 cm (2 in) and cut. Fold a strip in half, and sew this to the drawn oval line. Repeat until the whole oval joins up, and then using this process fill until there is roughly a 3 cm (1½ in) area left.

5. Sew a tape that matches the other ribbons onto the sewn line to conceal it.

Note* Make sure the foot and needle placement of the sewing machine are on the left-hand side of the loop, and that you are sewing in an anti-clockwise direction, as on page 31.

ASSEMBLAGE

6

MATERIALS & EQUIPMENT

→ **Second-hand skirt, or about 2 m (2 yd) fabric for skirt base – use the pattern sheet provided**

→ 5 different or contrasting colours of Petersham tape, braid or ribbon

→ A string of Suffolk puffs or short lengths about 4 cm (1½ in) long

SEE ALSO
Making ties, pages 24-25
Making tags, page 31
Sewing into a seam, page 32
Making a Suffolk puff, page 33

One day a package turned up in the post, sent from an old school teacher. It contained Petersham tape, ribbon, Suffolk puffs, 1950s buttons and 1920s closures. This skirt is the result of that fortunate windfall.

1. Cut out and make your skirt (see pages 8-27), or reclaim a skirt from a charity shop.

2. Take the Petersham and cut into 30 tags approximately 6 cm (2¼ in) long. Cut the Suffolk puff string into short lengths, about 4 cm (1½ in) long.

3. Lay the skirt on a flat surface and find the centreline, then with the tailor's chalk, make a mark 10-12 cm (4-5 in) to one side, at the top and bottom edges. Using a measuring tape or yard stick as a guide, draw a line vertically down the centre of the skirt, cut the skirt in half then fold the skirt so the right sides are facing.

4. Starting at the waistband of the skirt, take a tag of Petersham and fold it in half. Lay the tag into the seam with the two loose ends on the seam line. Alternate

Suffolk puffs with the tags. Add another tag so that it overlaps the one before. Continue like this until you reach the hem. Lay the other side of the skirt on top of the tags and puffs, right sides together, and sew with a 1 cm (³⁄₈ in) allowance to secure the seam. Press the seam flat.

5. Lay the skirt on a flat surface and make another cut and seam about 5 cm (2 in) to one side of the one you have just made. Repeat these steps 4 times, taking care not to catch the tags in the seam – they should be flat and facing away from the sewing machine. You should end up with 5 strips of tags.

6. Add your lining fabric, catching the top edges of the tags into the seam. Make extra long ties in the same fabric as the lining to fasten the skirt and hang down at the sides.

SISTER

7

MATERIALS & EQUIPMENT

→ **Second-hand skirt, or about 2 m (2 yd) fabric for skirt base – use the pattern sheet provided**

→ Virtually any type of tape you can find: ribbon, Petersham tape, cotton tape, satin tape, polyester tape, shoelaces, chains or zips

SEE ALSO
Making loops, page 30

TIP
All of the raw edges will be covered by the layers on top. The final layer will be absorbed into the seam of the lining.

This is sister to a skirt originally inspired by a box of shoelaces, found in a second-hand shop near Heathrow Airport. I was later given an image of a man from South America selling shoelaces: he was covered in at least a thousand pairs – many different colours, patterns and textures in multiples. This skirt is my homage to him.

1. Cut out and make your skirt (see pages 8-27), or reclaim a skirt from a charity shop.

2. Draw a line in tailor's chalk 2 cm (¾ in) above the hemline all the way around the bottom of the skirt.

3. Cut the tapes into lengths of 40 cm (15½ in). Take a strip, and with the pattern facing outwards, fold it in half to make a loop. Sew this to the line and repeat until the whole line is full.

4. Draw a parallel line 2 cm (¾ in) from where your original line was, and repeat step 3. Continue until the whole skirt is full.

LOVE CIRCLE

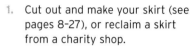

MATERIALS & EQUIPMENT

→ **Second-hand skirt, or about 2 m (2 yd) fabric for skirt base – use the pattern sheet provided**

→ Circle template A from pattern sheet

→ Heavy paper for template

→ Ribbon, Petersham tape, ripped strips of any fabric, cotton tape, satin tape and polyester tape

→ Sealing wax

→ Large brooch or adornment

SEE ALSO
Making tags, page 31

TIP
Sealing wax was the old-fashioned way of closing a letter before adhesive envelopes were invented. Why not try using it? It usually comes as a hard stick. Hold the stick in one hand and melt it over the flame of an ordinary match or lighter. The wax will drip down onto your chosen target.

A letter that I found in an antique shop was the inspiration for this skirt. Melted onto the back of the envelope was a large wax seal, with a beautiful stamp indented in it. Then I found a box of sealing wax in my Granny's attic and the rest is history.

1. Cut out and make your skirt (see pages 8-27), or reclaim a skirt from a charity shop.

2. Make a circle template so that the diameter measures 10 cm (4 in) less than the length of the skirt. Lay the skirt on a flat surface and mark the centreline. Place the large circle template on the skirt so that it is 5 cm (2 in) from the top and bottom edges and to one side of the central line. Use tailor's chalk to draw around it.

3. Cut your ribbon, tape and strips to 8 cm (3⅛ in) lengths. Fold these in half, placing the raw edges so they point inwards, and sew them to the chalk line. Continue around the circle until they join up.

4. To start the next circle measure 1 cm (⅜ in) inside the raw edges of the ribbon. Repeat step 3 until you have a circle in the middle approximately 2 cm (⅜ in) in diameter.

5. Drip sealing wax all over the centre of the looped ruffle and allow the wax to harden before attaching your brooch.

LAYERING

Much of the inspiration for my work comes from the inner city where I have my studio: lanes, alleys, passages, streets and terraces. Places that are neglected, ever-changing, disintegrating and subsiding spark ideas — crumbling walls, fly posters laid one on top of each other, weathered peeling paint, marks and stains. A kaleidoscope of colour, texture, tone, scale, shape, pattern, line and placement — in short, a mass of layers.

This is interpreted by layering fabric samples; one on top of the other, then cutting shapes out of them. These are then sewn down the middle and opened out to create a three-dimensional object, which is sewn into position on a skirt.

Below: Some of the images that have inspired my designs. I record images on a camera or with a sketchbook, then refer back to them when I am looking for ideas.

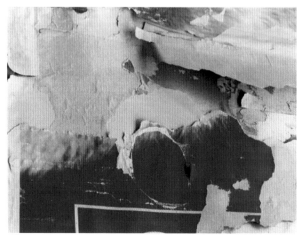

CUTTING AND STITCHING LAYERED SHAPES

1 Layer leftover pieces of fabric one on top of the other, two to eleven layers of fabric deep. To avoid wasting fabric later on, make sure your fabric leftovers are roughly the same size. Place a simply shaped template – a circle, or diamond, for example – on the edge of the fabric pile. Using tailor's chalk, draw around the shape. Move the template along and draw around it again, until you have a row of shapes.

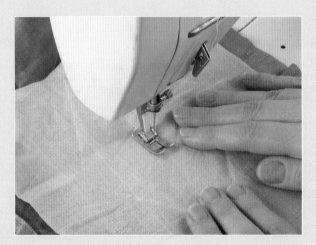

2 Sew a straight line through the pile of fabric, passing through the centre of each drawn shape.

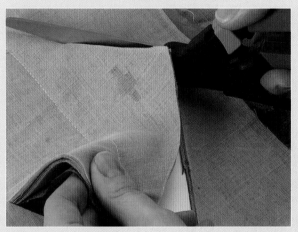

3 Once you have sewn all the layers together, cut out the shapes, cutting through all of the layers.

4 Separate the layers in each piece so that they fluff up.

BLIZZARD

9

MATERIALS & EQUIPMENT

→ **Second-hand skirt, or about 2 m (2 yd) fabric for skirt base – use the pattern sheet provided**

→ Different-toned and patterned fabric leftovers of the same general colour

→ Diamond template F from pattern sheet

→ Heavy paper for template

SEE ALSO
Inspiration, page 10
Cutting and stitching layered shapes, page 49

TIP
This skirt uses various red shades and patterns. Confining the design to one colour enables you to create a harmonious result.

The exhibition 'Stars, stripes, and spirals: Quilts from Wales and America' at The American Museum in Bath, England, inspired these geometric patterns and layers. Patchwork is a technique that demands patience – the technique you use to make this skirt is like patchwork, but much easier and quicker.

1. Cut out and make your skirt (see pages 8-27), or reclaim a skirt from a charity shop. Make sure your fabric leftovers are roughly the same size – this creates less waste later on.

2. Layer the leftovers one on top of the other, five-layers deep. Using the large diamond template as a guide, make a diamond out of heavy paper and follow the instuctions for cutting out layers, page 49.

3. Draw out twenty large diamonds and cut them out – you can do more later on if you need to. Repeat this process using the small diamond template.

4. When all the diamonds are cut out, use tailor's chalk to mark a dot on the skirt where you would like to see the first cluster of diamonds. Take a large diamond fabric piece and place the top point on the dot of tailor's chalk and pin in place. To secure the pile to the skirt, start at the outside point of the diamond, and use running, or machine stitch to sew down the middle, following the already sewn line. When you get to the end, leave the needle in the fabric, take a small diamond and place it next to the large diamond. Sew up and back along the small diamond, so that you finish at the join of the two diamonds.

5. Work a whole diamond cluster in this way, using six diamonds for each star. Repeat these steps for the rest of the skirt. If you think you need more diamond clusters, lay the skirt out flat, and mark more dots with the tailor's chalk.

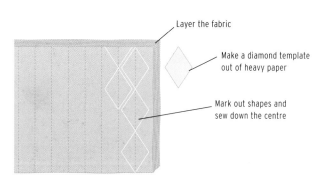

Layer the fabric

Make a diamond template out of heavy paper

Mark out shapes and sew down the centre

ARMCHAIR

10

MATERIALS & EQUIPMENT

→ **Second-hand skirt, or about 2 m (2 yd) fabric for skirt base – use the pattern sheet provided**

→ Heavy paper for template

→ Circle template A from pattern sheet

→ Matching, different-toned and patterned fabric leftovers

SEE ALSO
Cutting and stitching layered shapes, page 49

Layering is a good technique if you want to create a three-dimensional surface that allows you to show off both sides of the fabric. These upholstery tweeds left over from covering an armchair, for instance, have a lovely woven texture that is visible on the reverse side as well.

1. Cut out and make your skirt (see pages 8-27), or reclaim a skirt from a charity shop.

2. Make a large circle template, so that the diameter measures 10 cm (4 in) less than the length of the skirt.

3. Lay the skirt on a flat surface and mark the centreline. Place the circle template on the skirt so that it is 5 cm (2 in) from the top and bottom edges, and the outside edge is on the central line. Use tailor's chalk to draw around it.

4. Layer the patterned leftovers one on top of the other to create a pile of fabric three-layers deep. Using a smaller circle template measuring 10 cm (4 in) in diameter, mark the middle of the circle and sew a straight line from the top to the bottom through all layers.

5. Place the small circle template so that the central top and bottom points are directly on the sewn line, and draw around it. Draw out 50 circles and cut them out – you can do more if you need them.

6. Take a fabric circle and sew it to the chalk line, following the line already sewn. Fill the chalk circle. Sew a second line of circles flush to the first line of circles. Repeat, until you reach the centre. Sew one circle in the centre to finish.

AROUND & AROUND

MATERIALS & EQUIPMENT

→ **Second-hand skirt, or about 2 m (2 yd) fabric for skirt base – use the pattern sheet provided**

→ Circle template A from pattern sheet

→ Heavy paper for template

→ Matching, different-toned and patterned fabric leftovers

This uses the same idea as Armchair, but here the circles are arranged in a large star shape. The background is dark and shiny, so the design shows up more as a single motif.

1. Cut out and make your skirt (see pages 8–27), or reclaim a skirt from a charity shop.

2. Make fifty circles 5 cm (2 in) in diameter with the template, in the same way as for Armchair, using fabric five-layers deep.

3. Measure approximately 30 cm (12 in) up from the hemline, either to the left or right of the centre of the skirt. Place your first disc here, and sew this onto the skirt, along the stitch line.

4. Sew a circle of 6 discs around the first disc, and repeat twice more with 12 discs. Space the next circle out more, placing a disc next to alternate discs in the round before, to create a radiating star shape.

REMAINDERED

12

MATERIALS & EQUIPMENT

→ **Second-hand skirt, or about 2 m (2 yd) fabric for skirt base – use the pattern sheet provided**

→ Circle template A from pattern sheet

→ Heavy paper for template

→ Matching, different-toned and patterned fabric leftovers

TIP

Attach the lining before the last round of segments are added to allow the points to make a dramatic edging, or catch the tips in the seam to make a neat edge.

These circles were left over from another project. The pale colours and white fabrics, and the different types of fabrics and textures, enhance the floaty, ethereal impression.

1. Cut out and make your skirt (see pages 8-27), or reclaim a skirt from a charity shop.

2. Make 100 fabric circles with minimum diameter of 25 cm (10 in) using the circle template. You can cut more if you need to.

3. Draw a line in tailor's chalk 2 cm (³/₈ in) up from the hemline, all the way around the bottom of the skirt.

4. Take a circle and fold it in half, and then fold it in half again, to make a quarter circle. Sew the tip of the shape to the line and repeat until the whole line is full.

5. Draw another line 2 cm (³/₈ in) up from the original line, towards the waistband and following around the skirt again, repeat step 3, until the whole skirt is full. At the final round of segments, make sure the points of the segments are even as they will be seen.

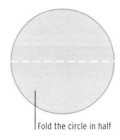
Fold the circle in half

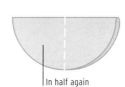
In half again

And in half again

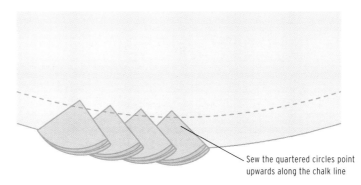
Sew the quartered circles point upwards along the chalk line

KATHRYN WHEEL I

13

MATERIALS & EQUIPMENT

→ **Second-hand skirt, or about 2 m (2 yd) fabric for skirt base – use the pattern sheet provided**

→ Large diamond template F from pattern sheet

→ Heavy paper for template

→ Eight different-patterned, coloured and textured leftover fabrics that complement the skirt base

→ Buttons in a complementary colour to the leftover fabric

TIP

To save time when cutting out shapes, layer the fabric, pin and cut through several layers at once, as many as you can without distorting the fabrics.

This skirt uses the diamond template again, but it is manipulated into a different shape, looking remarkably like patchwork, but without all the hard work.

1. Cut out and make your skirt (see pages 8–27), or reclaim a skirt from a charity shop.

2. Transfer the large diamond template to heavy paper and cut out. Use this template to draw out thirty large diamonds in the fabric and cut them out. You can do more if you need them.

3. Once you have cut the diamonds out, hold your skirt up and look in a mirror. Using tailor's chalk, mark a dot where you would like to see the first cluster.

4. Take a large fabric diamond, fold it in half and place the point on the dot of tailor's chalk.

5. Starting at the outside edge, use running stitch to sew towards the point, and back to the start. Leave the needle in the fabric, take another folded diamond and place its points next to the first points, like a segment of a cake. Sew up and back along the diamond, so that you finish at the join of the two diamonds (see opposite).

6. Work a whole cluster in this way, using six diamonds for each Kathryn wheel. Repeat these steps for the rest of the skirt. If you think you need more Kathryn wheels, put the skirt on again, and mark more dots with the tailor's chalk.

KATHRYN WHEEL II

14

MATERIALS & EQUIPMENT

→ **Second-hand skirt, or about 2 m (2 yd) fabric for skirt base – use the pattern sheet provided**

→ Small diamond template F from pattern sheet

→ Heavy paper for template

→ Eight different-patterned, coloured and textured leftover fabrics that complement the skirt base

→ Contrasting buttons

TIP
If you can't find enough matching buttons that suit your material, you can cover your own. Self-cover buttons come in a variety of sizes and you can blend them with your project perfectly.

This skirt is worked in the same way as Kathryn Wheel 1, using smaller diamonds and contrasting buttons.

1. Use the small diamond template to cut out your initial shapes.

2. Repeat the steps in Kathryn Wheel 1.

3. Finish each cluster or wheel with a small button at its centre.

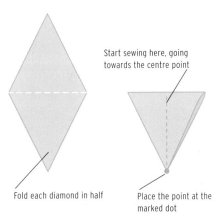

Fold each diamond in half

Start sewing here, going towards the centre point

Place the point at the marked dot

Place six diamonds with their points meeting in the centre

SUSHI ROLLS

15

MATERIALS & EQUIPMENT

→ **Second-hand skirt, or about 2 m (2 yd) fabric for skirt base – use the pattern sheet provided**

→ Circle template A from pattern sheet

→ Heavy paper for template

→ Extra fabric from skirt base and brightly patterned coloured silk

SEE ALSO

Cutting and stitching layered shapes, page 49

The Japanese seem to get the style so right for packaging, food and presentation. One skirt that I was working on had layered fabric discs, which proved problematic as the skirt was so flat. While eating some sushi, I looked at the food in the restaurant and thought, why not roll the fabric?

1. Cut out and make your skirt (see pages 8-27), or reclaim a skirt from a charity shop.

2. Make a circle template so that the diameter measures 10 cm (4 in) less than the length of the skirt. Lay the skirt on a flat surface and mark the centreline. Place the large circle template on the skirt so that it is 5 cm (2 in) from the top and bottom edges and to one side of the central line. Use tailor's chalk to draw around it.

3. Layer the leftovers to create a pile 2-layers deep and sew a straight line along the centre.

4. Make a template from the smaller circle 10 cm (4 in) in diameter. Place the circle template on the centre of the sewn line, and draw around it. Draw out fifty circles and cut them out – you can do more later on if you need them.

5. Take a fabric circle, roll it and sew it to the chalk line along its already sewn line, so that the last bit of rolled circle has its back to the sewing machine foot (see below). Fill the chalk-line circle.

6. Sew a second line of circles flush to the first line, and repeat two more times.

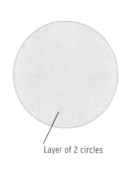

Layer of 2 circles

Roll the circle like this

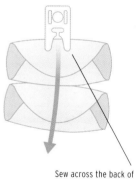

Sew across the back of the folded edge like this

SIMPLE SUSHI

16

MATERIALS & EQUIPMENT

→ **Second-hand skirt, or about 2 m (2 yd) fabric for skirt base – use the pattern sheet provided**

→ Circle template A from pattern sheet

→ Heavy paper for template

→ Extra fabric from skirt base and brightly patterned, coloured silks and cottons

SEE ALSO
Cutting and stitching layered shapes, page 49
Sushi rolls, page 58

This is a dramatic, but simplified version of the original sushi skirt, with fewer rolls and more circles. If you are inspired, fill the circles with more rolls.

1. Cut out and make your skirt (see pages 8-27), or reclaim a skirt from a charity shop.

2. Lay the skirt on a flat surface. Make a circle template, with a diameter measuring approximately 30 cm (12 in).

3. Mark roughly 3 to 5 circles on the skirt base, with a gap of about 5 cm (2 in) in between them, making sure at least one runs off the edge of the hemline or waistband.

4. Layer the leftovers 2-layers deep and sew a straight line along the centre (see cutting and stitching layered shapes, page 49).

5. Make a template from the smaller circle 10 cm (4 in) in diameter. Place the circle template on the centre of the sewn line, and draw around it. Draw out fifty circles and cut them out – you can do more later on if you need them.

6. Take a fabric circle, roll it and sew it to the chalk line you marked out on the skirt base, taking care to sew along its already sewn line, so that the last bit of rolled circle has its back to the sewing machine foot.

7. Fill the chalk line circle. Repeat for the rest of the circles.

USING FOUND OBJECTS

Car boot sales and second-hand or charity shops where you can gather materials and embellishments can be a real addiction. Second-hand shops and flea markets are great sources when looking for a bargain. There's nothing quite like the joy of finding a box full of buttons or some unusual, ornate fabric.

It is a delight using materials that have marks on them from previous lives: 1950s patterns and colours, old-fashioned typefaces, beautifully made packaging – no cheap plastic – and wonderfully crafted materials. Attics can be a treasure trove of wonderful old things: mothers and grandmothers are a spectacular source of 1920s, 1950s, or 1960s garments, fabrics and notions.

If people find out you are collecting all these types of fabrics and notions, you may receive donations – bags of ribbon, or shoeboxes full of buttons through the mail, each bursting with inspiration. It can be the highlight of the month when such a package arrives with the postman.

NEW TECHNIQUES WITH OLD MATERIALS

The one rule about found and recycled materials is that you have to use them, or lose them. Go on and cut them up, or sew through them. What is the point in having boxes, tins, and drawers full of vinatge finds, if you have no use for them?

Don't stop at collecting traditional sewing materials. Found objects that are glass, plastic, wood, ceramic, rubber and paper should be celebrated.

BUTTONS
Buttons are a traditional closure, but can be used for purely decorative purposes. They come in a wonderful array of shapes, sizes and colours – some elaborately designed, but even plain buttons can look luscious if you use enough of them together.

Sew on buttons exactly as you would sew one onto a shirt. Secure the thread end in the fabric and take the needle through one of the buttonholes from the wrong side to the right side. Take the needle back down through the other hole, and through the fabric. Make several stitches between each hole, making a bar, or two bars if there are four holes. Secure the thread at the back of the fabric, or move straight on to the next button.

BEADS

Sewing beads, sequins or any multiples of small embellishments to your skirt will add texture and drama. Use lines of beads to create marks, patterns and designs on the fabric, and to add colour if required.

When attaching beads, use a long, fine beading needle, that will fit through the hole in the beads with ease. Secure the thread at the back of the work, and then thread the beads onto the needle. Make a line, shape or pattern with the line of beads, and insert the thread back into the material. Bring the needle back up along the line of beads, making stitches between the beads to hold the line in place.

STUDS

In much the same way as buttons, studs can be used to embellish as well as fasten. No-sew studs and snaps come in various sizes. Some upholstery studs have spikes that can be pushed through the fabric and folded over on the reverse. Two-part studs are often used for work clothes or camping equipment. The two parts are clamped into position through the layers of fabric, and are available in a pack with full instructions.

Choose the position of the stud, and pierce the fabric with the sharp end of the stud from the back. Place the other part of the stud over the top, and using a wooden board to protect the table, hit with a hammer until the two parts are securely fixed.

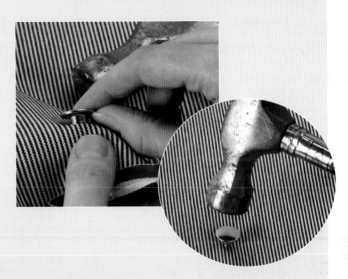

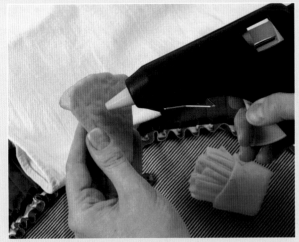

USING PLASTICS

The easiest way to attach plastics securely is with a glue gun. These are notoriously messy, so be sure to use a cloth to protect your work and table.

Decide on the position, place the gun on the back of the object to be stuck and squeeze the trigger to dab glue onto the object, then stick it down. Hold it in position for about 15 seconds to dry.

TIP

When using a glue gun, even if you are very careful, you may find that strands of glue spill onto your skirt. If this happens, put the whole skirt in the freezer for a few moments – the glue strands will become brittle and fall off.

TIE SILKS

17

MATERIALS & EQUIPMENT

→ **Second-hand skirt, or about 2 m (2 yd) fabric for skirt base – use the pattern sheet provided**

→ Old ties

→ Large diamond template F from pattern sheet

→ Heavy paper for template

→ Leftover pieces of fabric from the skirt base

→ Buttons

SEE ALSO
Deconstruction, pages 12-13
Cutting and stitching layered shapes, page 49

TIP
Take into consideration the base fabric of the skirt when selecting the colour and pattern of ties. Here we chose black and red.

Men's ties provide such a wide selection of patterned, coloured, and textured fabric. When using a mixture of ties, you get a variation of fabric, colour and shape because you only have a small amount of each fabric.

1. Cut out and make your skirt (see pages 8-27), or reclaim a skirt from a charity shop.

2. Pick apart the seams on your chosen ties and iron flat, making sure the diamond template fits onto each piece of fabric.

3. Lay ties onto leftover pieces of fabric from the skirt base. Sew through both layers down the centre of the tie silks. Place the diamond template so that both the top and bottom points are directly on the sewn line, and draw around it. Draw out twenty diamonds and cut them out – you can do more if you need them.

4. When all the diamonds are cut out, take your tailor's chalk and mark a dot on the skirt where you would like to see the first cluster of diamonds. Take a diamond, and with the silk facing upwards, place the top point on the dot of tailor's chalk. Start at the bottom point and, following the already sewn line, use running stitch to sew down the middle and hold the diamond in place. When you get to the end, leave the needle in the fabric, take another diamond and place it next to the first diamond. Sew up and back along the diamond, so that you finish at the join of both diamonds.

5. Work a whole diamond cluster in this way, using six diamonds. Repeat these steps for the rest of the skirt. If you think you need more diamond clusters, mark more dots with the tailor's chalk. Finish the centre of each cluster with a button.

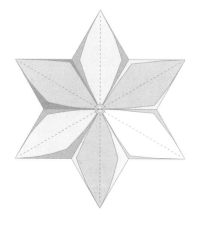

MAD HATTER

18

MATERIALS & EQUIPMENT

→ **Second-hand skirt, or about 2 m (2 yd) fabric for skirt base – use the pattern sheet provided**

→ Half a vintage skirt

→ Heavy paper for stencil

→ Circle template A from pattern sheet

→ 10-12 button badges

→ Hat silk or lining of old hat

SEE ALSO
Deconstruction, pages 12-13
Making a stencil and using a silkscreen, page 83

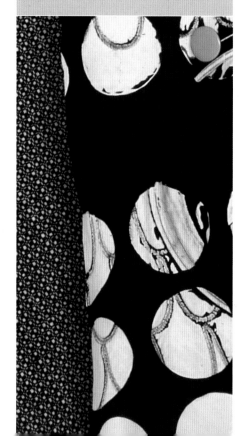

In the middle of Marlborough, Wiltshire, a bag of hat silks was discovered in the discount back room of an antique shop that used to be a church. A milliner in Manchester had made them to line hats, and the typeface on the silks was decorative enough to use the fabric as the surface for a skirt.

1. Cut out and make your skirt (see pages 8-27), or reclaim a skirt from a charity shop.

2. Cut the vintage skirt in half along the seams, and sew one piece to the waistband of the new skirt, so the vintage skirt will sit either on the left or right side. Sew your hat silk onto the lower half of the vintage skirt.

3. Make a paper stencil by repeating the smallest circle from template A on the pattern sheet. Lay the skirt out flat, and print with a blank screen and spotty paper stencil all over the skirt, including the hat silk and vintage skirt.

4. Once dry, add the button badges in a line down the skirt front and add your lining.

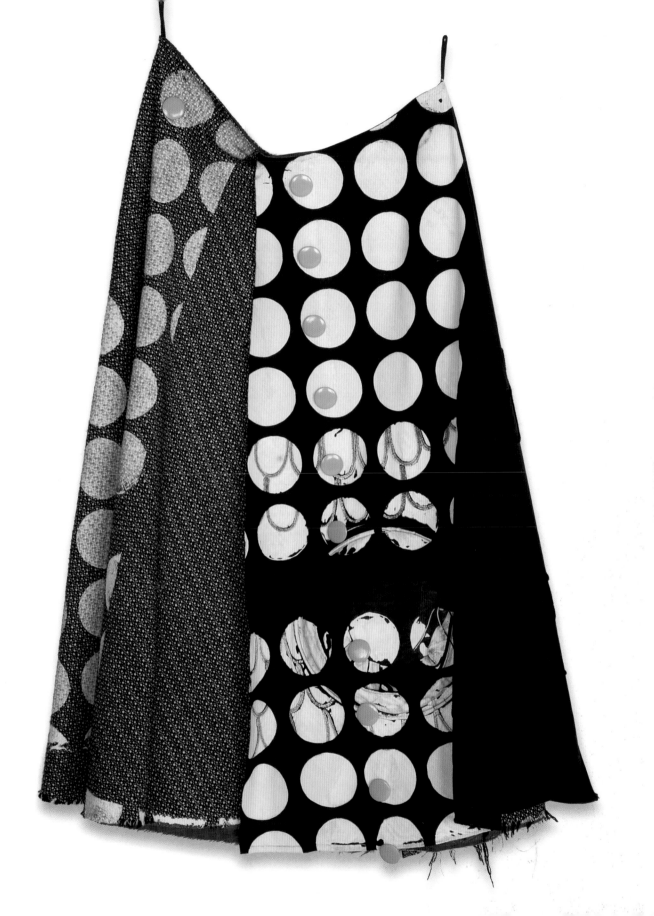

TAPESTRY

19

MATERIALS & EQUIPMENT

→ **Second-hand skirt, or about
 2 m (2 yd) fabric for skirt
 base – use the pattern sheet
 provided**

→ Old tapestries

→ Fusible webbing

→ Heavy paper for stencil (using
 a stencil of your choice)

SEE ALSO
Using found objects, page 60

Making a stencil and using
a silkscreen, page 83

Using fusible webbing, page 99

Tapestries of cottages, countryside and ballerinas are very
popular. The task: to put them onto fabric but without seeing
the design so literally. The solution: cutting them into a grid
and attaching them in a grid, a tapestry within a tapestry.

1. Cut out and make your skirt (see
 pages 8–27), or reclaim a skirt
 from a charity shop.

2. Print the skirt using a paper
 stencil in a pattern of your
 choice (see page 83), and leave
 to dry.

3. Meanwhile, using an iron, cover
 the back of the tapestry in
 fusible webbing to secure the
 stitches of the tapestries.

4. Cut the tapestries into equal-
 sized squares – divide them
 exactly so there are no leftovers.
 Make a square template, so that

the diameter measures 10 cm
(4 in) less than the length of
the skirt.

4. Lay the skirt on a flat surface
 and mark the centreline. Place
 the square template on the skirt
 so that it is 5 cm (2 in) from the
 top and bottom edges and to
 one side of the central line. Use
 tailor's chalk to draw around it.

5. With a 0.5 cm ($^3/_{16}$ in) gap
 between them, sew your
 tapestry squares around the
 edges to the template chalk line.
 Repeat until you fill your square.
 Attach a lining to finish the skirt.

BLACK & WHITE VINTAGE

MATERIALS & EQUIPMENT

→ **Second-hand skirt, or about 2 m (2 yd) fabric for skirt base – use the pattern sheet provided**

→ Another second-hand or old skirt

→ Leftover fabrics that complement the skirt base

→ Oval template G from pattern sheet

→ Heavy paper for template

→ Buttons

SEE ALSO
Cutting and stitching layered shapes, page 49

TIP
People seem to be getting larger, so vintage skirts will often be too small to wear, so cut them up and use them again.

This is half a 1960s circle skirt, mixing new and vintage together to create a new skirt. The old skirt is used as if it were a giant piece of appliqué. How your skirt looks will depend on the vintage skirt you can find.

1. Cut out and make your skirt (see pages 8-27), or reclaim a skirt from a charity shop.

2. Open out the other reclaimed skirt in half using a seam as a cutting line, and sew to the waistband of the new skirt, so that the vintage skirt will sit either on the left or right leg when worn.

3. Layer the leftover fabric in 2 layers. Sew a line through the centre (see cutting through layers, page 98).

4. Next, place the oval template so that the top and bottom points are directly on the sewn line, and draw around it. Draw out 15 ovals and cut them out – you can do more if you need them. Sew 3 or 5 clusters of ovals onto the vintage skirt as shown.

5. Just under the vintage skirt, draw 2 circles and stitch on buttons. Add more flower clusters on the base skirt.

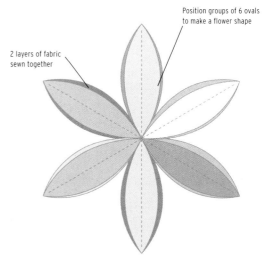

Position groups of 6 ovals to make a flower shape

2 layers of fabric sewn together

BADGES

21

MATERIALS & EQUIPMENT

→ **Second-hand skirt, or about 2 m (2 yd) fabric for skirt base – use the pattern sheet provided**

→ Circle template A from pattern sheet

→ Heavy paper for template

→ A colourful selection of 2.5 cm (1 in) badges

TIP
If you don't have a stash of old badges, buy some online.

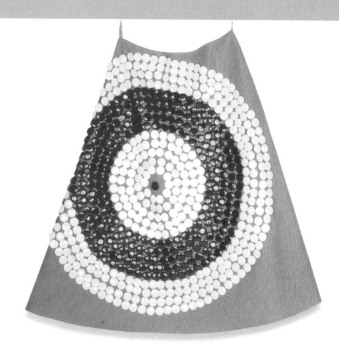

Button badges are objects you can collect over a period of time, in different sizes, shapes and patterns – they always seem to gather at the bottom of drawers. Imagine the beautifully smooth texture of a complete surface of shiny badges and the noise it makes when you walk down the street.

1. Cut out your skirt and make (see pages 8-27), or reclaim a skirt from a charity shop.

2. Make a circle template, so that the diameter measures 10 cm (4 in) less than the length of the skirt.

3. Lay the skirt on a flat surface and mark the centreline. Place the circle template on the skirt so that it is 5 cm (2 in) from the top and bottom edges, and to one side of the central line. Use tailor's chalk to draw around it.

4. Attach the badges to the drawn line so there are no gaps between each badge. In order to get a smooth line, this may take some jostling about.

5. When the circle line is full, start the next line of badges, working inward and using the line of badges as a guide. Continue until the badges come full circle.

BUTTONS

22

MATERIALS & EQUIPMENT

→ **Second-hand skirt, or about 2 m (2 yd) fabric for skirt base – use the pattern sheet provided**

→ Transfer foil

→ Large circle template A from pattern sheet

→ Heavy paper for template

→ Every single button you own, or use someone else's

SEE ALSO
Using found objects, pages 60-61
Transfer foiling, page 83

Boxes, tins and drawers full of buttons are hidden away in every household. Sometimes it is cathartic to have a clean out, so load up a skirt with buttons.

1. Cut out your skirt and make (see pages 8-27), or reclaim a skirt from a charity shop.

2. Paint glue onto the skirt base using a large brush, then apply transfer foil in a complementary metallic colour.

3. Make a large circle template, with a diameter 10 cm (4 in) less than the length of the skirt. Place the skirt on a flat surface with the template 5 cm (2 in) from the top and bottom edges, and to one side of the central line. Use tailor's chalk to draw around it.

4. Starting at the outside edge of the circle, sew buttons on by hand. Make sure the thread you sew with is thick and doubled up, for extra security. Keep sewing, keeping the buttons close together until you run out of buttons.

GREEN GROCER

23

MATERIALS & EQUIPMENT

→ **Second-hand skirt, or about 2 m (2 yd) heavyweight fabric for skirt base – use the pattern sheet provided**

→ Large circle template A from pattern sheet

→ Heavy paper for template

→ Plastic fruit, vegetables and packaging material

→ An assortment of artificial flowers, foliage and feathers

→ Glue gun

SEE ALSO
Using plastics, page 61

Silk flowers and bags of children's play food are readily available at your local charity shop. The colours and textures look great together, so why not put them on a skirt? A cream canvas makes the colours stand out, and the weight of all the objects and materials will be supported by the weave of the canvas.

1. Cut out and make your skirt (see pages 8-27), or reclaim a skirt from a charity shop.

2. Make a circle template, so that the diameter measures 10 cm (4 in) less than the skirt.

3. Lay the skirt on a flat surface and mark the centreline. Place the circle template on the skirt so that it is 5 cm (2 in) from the top and bottom edges, and to one side of the central line. Use tailor's chalk to draw around it.

4. Attach the flowers and food onto the circle using the chalk line as a guide to start you. Use a glue gun to attach plastics, securing with needle and thread where possible. Continue until the circle is full, or just leave areas of fabric to show – negative space or plain fabric can be just as good as a patterned surface.

HATPINS

24

MATERIALS & EQUIPMENT

→ **Second-hand skirt, or about 2 m (2 yd) fabric for skirt base – use the pattern sheet provided**

→ Contrasting fabric for loops

→ Hatpins with stoppers

Antique shops are full of the most exquisite costume jewellery and hatpins. The head of one pin I came across had a circle carved with a red and cream pattern on it. Buying vintage hatpins is now quite difficult and expensive, annoying when you have such a fetish for them, so collect them whenever you see them. If you can't find hatpins, make a similar design with safety, or kilt pins.

SEE ALSO

Making loops, page 30
Sewing fabric into seams, page 32

1. Cut out and make your skirt (see pages 8-27), or reclaim a skirt from a charity shop.

2. Take the fabric for your loops and tear into 30 strips, 56 cm (22 in) long, 2 cm (³/₄ in) wide. Remove any excess threads from the strips and iron flat.

3. Lay the skirt on a flat surface, find the centreline then make a mark 10-12 cm (4-5 in) to one side with the tailor's chalk at the top and bottom edges. Using a measuring tape or yard stick as a guide, draw a line vertically down the centre of the skirt. Next, cut the skirt in half, and then fold the skirt so the right sides are facing.

4. Starting at the waistband of the skirt, take a strip of fabric and fold it in half. Insert the fabric into the seam with the two loose ends on the seam line and pin. Add another loop of fabric so that it overlaps the first loop, continuing until you reach the hem (see page 32).

5. Sew the two pieces of skirt together with a 1 cm (³/₈ in) seam allowance, including all loops into the seam. Press the seam and loops flat and backtack to secure the seam. Be sure to account for the loss of width caused by cutting the skirt apart and sewing it together.

6. Put on the skirt, mark where you would like the pins to sit (you don't really want to be sitting on them). Take off the skirt and apply the pins to the skirt in a star, as shown in the diagram below.

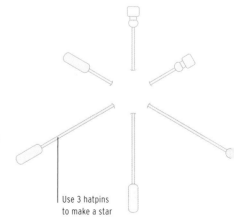

Use 3 hatpins to make a star

BOY'S OWN

25

MATERIALS & EQUIPMENT

→ **Second-hand skirt, or about 2 m (2 yd) fabric for skirt base – use the pattern sheet provided**

→ Letters template C on pattern sheet, or different typefaces enlarged on a photocopier to make your own words

→ Different types of writing utensils: pencils, fibre-tip or ballpoint pens, permanent markers of different widths

→ Embroidery floss

→ White glue

→ Coloured sand, beads, studs and other found objects

SEE ALSO

Using found objects, pages 60-61
Mark making, pages 80-83
Running stitch, page 81

TIP

Make the outlines of your chosen word in similar colours, so that it doesn't become too busy. When you are drawing the line, don't just think of a straight line, use spotted lines, filling in lines, running lines. If using calico or canvas, make sure you wash it first, as it then has a soft rather than stiff texture so it will be easier to work with. If you use sand you won't be able to wash it afterwards.

In a photo of the boys' only entrance to a Victorian school, the word 'boys' stood out because of the boldness of the letters – they were more like geometric shapes than words. Here the word is used as a shape in repetition in all different found objects, stitches and marks to create a layered surface of textures. You could use any word you like. The inks used will fade over time to create an aged effect.

1. Cut out and make your skirt (see pages 8-27), or reclaim a skirt from a charity shop.

2. Lay out your skirt flat. In pencil, trace five (you can do more when you need to) 'boys' in different typefaces. To do this, print out the word using a computer, or cut out from a newspaper or magazine, and place underneath the fabric. If you can't see through, you can trace the outline with tracing paper, and transfer to the fabric.

3. Following the first 'boys' pencil line, take whatever media you like, for example beads, or embroidery stitches, and build up the lines. Then, for the next line, use a ballpoint pen or marker to go over the lines.

4. Use white glue to paint the outline of a word, then sprinkle sand over the top. Then use studs or beads to outline one of the words.

5. Continue like this until the whole skirt is layered and covered with different typefaces and layered textures of your chosen word.

ECLIPSE

26

MATERIALS & EQUIPMENT

→ **Second-hand skirt, or about 2 m (2 yd) fabric for skirt base – use the pattern sheet provided**
→ Flower template E and circle template A from pattern sheet
→ Heavy paper for stencil
→ Silkscreen and squeegee
→ Embroidery hoop (optional)
→ Studs with teeth

SEE ALSO
Using studs, page 61
Making a stencil and using a silkscreen, page 83

This skirt is printed onto a waffle texture – the fabric is woven into squares that go down into the fabric, so the printing picks up the texture. The studs used here are quite plain, but you can get very elaborate ones from fabric stores, or online.

1. Cut out and make your skirt (see pages 8-27), or reclaim a skirt from a charity shop.

2. Photocopy the flower template to the largest size your copier will allow, and cut them out with a sharp knife. This will act as a paper stencil for your print.

3. Print your skirt using a paper stencil as shown in the mark-making chapter, (see pages 80-83) with first a spot repeat and then the flower template.

4. Once the print is dry, put on the skirt and mark out where you would like the half circle of studs to appear on the surface. Take off the skirt. On the back of the skirt, under the mark you have made, use a pen to draw around an embroidery hoop or medium-sized circle approximately 20 cm (8 in) in diameter or make a template from circle A on pattern sheet.

5. Attach the studs to the line from the front, so that the edges of the studs are touching each other, and following the pen line, so they are showing on the skirt front. Bend the teeth in using your fingers or the back of an old metal spoon.

MARK MAKING

Making marks is a phrase most commonly used by artists when drawing, but don't be alarmed – when applied to skirts, these are mark-making exercises, and require only very basic skills.

Skirts in this section have been decorated using a range of mark-making techniques: silkscreen printing and paper stencils, transfer foiling, hand sewing and machine stitching.
Silkscreen printing can be very sophisticated. Here, we are not transferring images onto the screen, but using simple paper stencils and a blank screen. Similarly, hand embroidery can be fine and intricate, but here we are using it *en masse* to create abstract patterns, rather than on its own as one or two stitches.

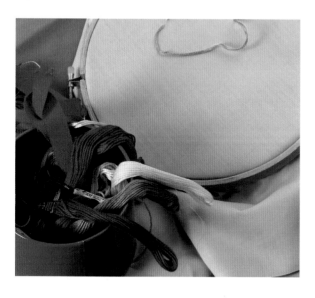

EMBROIDERY YARNS
Pretty much anything can be used to make a mark. Embroidery floss or tapestry wools are the traditional materials for embellishing fabrics. Knitting yarns, crochet cottons and any kind of string can also be used.

PENS
Fabric pens and pastels that fix permanently are expensive, so try using a fibre-tip pen, permanent marker or a ballpoint pen – all can be used to make marks. These may fade in light or after washing, but this really just adds to their charm.

FREEHAND X-STITCH

This isn't the counted thread work that dedicated embroiderers and cross-stitchers would recognise, but a more freehand version.

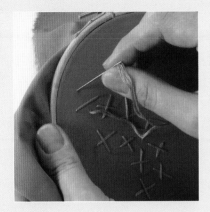 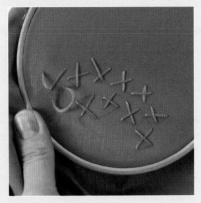 

1 Use a complementary coloured embroidery thread and sharp needle with a large eye. Hold the fabric in an embroidery hoop to keep it taut (see page 17).

2 Secure the thread at the back of the work, pull through to the front, and make a straight stitch.

3 Bring the thread back to the front and make another stitch that crosses the first one at right angles. Pull the thread tight from the other side, then bring the needle back to the front and make another stitch close to the last.

RUNNING STITCH

So far we have talked about buttons, studs, beads and other found objects as means of decorating fabric. Aside from such additions, thread itself can be used as part of the adornment process. Running stitch is a simple stitch that can be used to great effect to make patterns.

1 To create running stitch: hold the fabric in a large embroidery hoop (see page 17). Thread a long length of embroidery thread onto a long needle and then make several stabbing stitches, so that the gaps and the stitches are roughly the same length.

2 Pull the thread through and continue following the circle of the hoop until the circle is complete. Continue with another circle close to the last one.

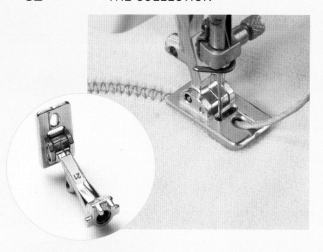

USING A CORDING FOOT

This is a machine stitch that uses a special foot, generally used to gather heavyweight fabrics or drapes. Here we have used it to create a decorative finish, where a thicker cord is held down with a zigzag stitch.

1 Change the foot on the sewing machine to a cording foot with a central hole (see changing a foot, page 15).

2 Thread piping or other cord through the hole in the foot, so the end is behind the machine. Set the machine to a wide and short zigzag stitch and stitch either side of the cord.

The cord will want to curve, so use this to create a pattern – curved edges are easier than corners. When you are ready to finish, cut the cord and stitch back and forth over the end to secure.

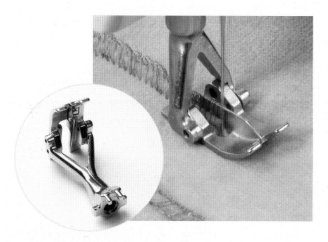

TAILOR TACKING STITCH

This is a technique used to transfer pattern markings to cut out fabric pieces, like darts, notches or pockets. Here it is used to make a surface pattern that is both textured and original.

1 Replace the usual foot on the machine with a tacking foot. This has a raised bar in the centre over which the stitches are forced.

2 Set the machine to a wide and short zigzag and work along in stripes, or create a pattern. A contrasting coloured thread emphasises the stitch – it is only the top thread that will show.

If you require a fluffier texture, try cutting the stitches down the centre. This will create a feathered look. The stitches will now be loose, so iron fusible webbing to the reverse to secure.

MAKING A STENCIL AND USING A SILKSCREEN

This is a very simple method of using a silkscreen to print an image. Fabric screen printing ink is the best ink to use, as it has the correct consistency. Use a hairdryer to speed dry, then iron on the reverse, protecting your ironing board with scrap paper. Fabric binding medium is also available to mix with your own pigments or inks.

1 Find a photograph, or an actual object that you want to copy – a flower or leaf are ideal.

TIP

Ready-made screens are available in good art stores, or online (see resources at the end of this book). If you cannot get hold of one, you can make your own by stapling some fine mesh fabric, such as undyed silk chiffon, to a sturdy wooden frame.

2 Photocopy the image and use a craft knife to cut around it. You are left with the negative – this is your stencil. Keep the shape that you have removed, as it may be useful as a template later on.

3 Place the stencil underneath a clean screen, covering any extra space on the screen with masking tape and more paper, or specialist screen filler. Place the printing ink at one end of the screen and spread the ink by pulling the squeegee towards you. Repeat until the image is clear. Clean the screen thoroughly after use.

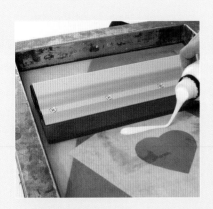

TRANSFER FOILING

1 Print your image through the screen with foiling glue and a stencil. Wash the screen. Allow the glue to dry before placing the the foil onto the glue, shiny side up.

2 Place a piece of newsprint on top of it and apply heat over it using an iron. Wait until the foil is totally cold, and then peel off the backing.

MONOCHROME GEOMETRY

27

MATERIALS & EQUIPMENT

→ **Second-hand skirt, or about 2 m (2 yd) fabric for skirt base – use the pattern sheet provided**

→ Circle template A from pattern sheet

→ Heavy paper for stencil

→ Silk screen and printing ink in black and white

→ Cording foot

→ Self-adhesive felt grips (used for putting under furniture)

Examine your own source images in great detail, with a viewfinder or magnifying glass. Look for colour, placement, shape, line, texture and scale. You can see the relationship between the images below and the geometric skirt that was inspired by them, opposite.

1. Cut out and make your skirt (see pages 8–27), or reclaim a skirt from a charity shop.

2. Lay the skirt out flat and using a blank screen, print it all black (unless the fabric is black already, that is).

3. When the print is dry, use the circle template to make a paper stencil with spots. Print white circles all over the black, moving the screen as you go, as the screen probably won't be big enough to cover the whole skirt.

4. When the skirt and paper stencil are dry, print circles in green ink over the skirt. Don't try to line up with the white circles, just print over them. Allow the ink to dry thoroughly, and press well on reverse.

5. Put on the skirt and chalk a mark where your left, or right thigh is. Take off the skirt. On the reverse, draw a circle roughly 32 cm (13 in) in diameter, around the mark you made on your thigh. With the cording foot, sew a spiral starting on the outside of the circle line, and finishing in the middle of the circle.

6. On either the left or right side of the skirt front, apply the square felt grips in a grid rectangle.

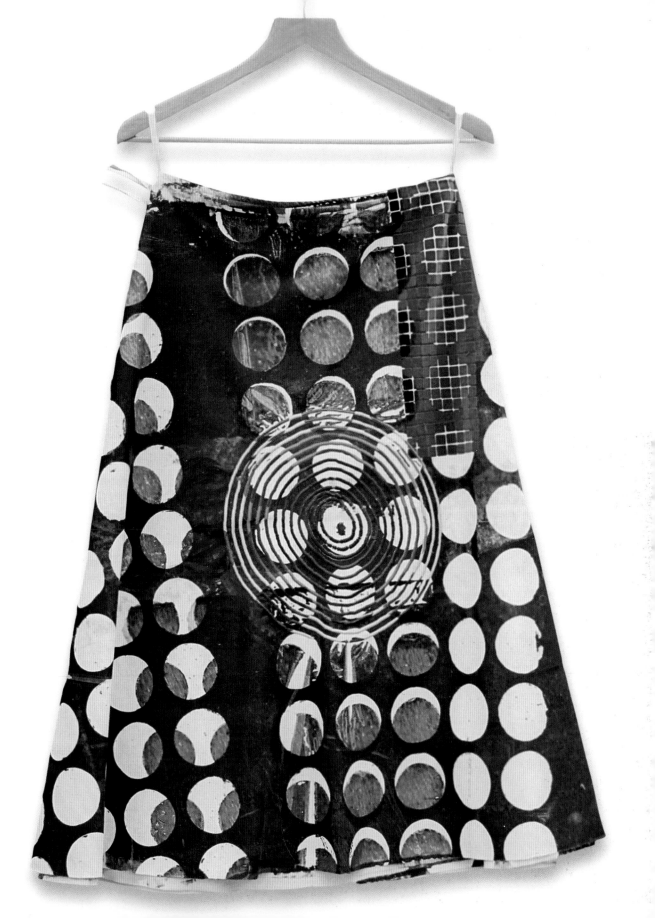

RUNNING IN CIRCLES

28

MATERIALS & EQUIPMENT

→ **Second-hand skirt, or about 2 m (2 yd) fabric for skirt base – use the pattern sheet provided**

→ Embroidery hoop – one large and one medium

→ Wool embroidery floss that is the same colour as the skirt, but different in tone, plus a complementary colour

Running stitch is a satisfyingly easy, relaxing technique. Simple techniques used *en masse* can look fantastic, so when this skirt is finished you will have a real sense of achievement.

SEE ALSO
Using an embroidery hoop, page 17

1. Cut out your skirt and make (see pages 8-27), or reclaim a skirt from a charity shop.

2. Take either the large or medium embroidery hoop and wherever you feel comfortable, attach it to the skirt, with the small circle at the back. Tighten the outer hoop and make sure the fabric is taut.

3. Using the hoop as a guide, and starting on the outside, sew a spiral inwards – it's easier to sew with a long needle so you can make several stitches at once. Allow a 1 cm ($^3/_8$ in) space between the stitches. For every circle there needs to be one row of stitches that is in a complementary colour, for example: red and green, blue and orange, purple and yellow or contrasting colours like black and white.

4. Move the hoop around and repeat, filling the skirt with circles. Finish the threads by sewing them in at the back of the work.

GREEN'S RUNNING STITCH

29

MATERIALS & EQUIPMENT

→ **Second-hand skirt, or about 2 m (2 yd) fabric for skirt base – use the pattern sheet provided**

→ Embroidery hoop – one large and one medium

→ Embroidery thread in toning colours

This is very similar to Running in Circles in technique (see opposite), although the effect is different. Previously the threads were a contrasting colour, here the colours are blending, with the texture against the shiny satin fabric emphasising the design.

TIP

When thinking of how many circles to sew, try using odd numbers 1, 3, 5, 7, 9, 11 and so on. This gives a sense that the made marks, prints or stitches are unintentional and random, so they won't look contrived.

1. Cut out your skirt and make (see pages 8-27), or reclaim a skirt from a charity shop.

2. Take either the large or medium embroidery hoop and wherever you feel comfortable, attach it to the skirt, with the small circle at the back. Tighten the outer hoop and make sure the fabric is taut.

3. Using the hoop as a guide, and starting on the outside, sew a spiral inwards – it's easier to sew with a long needle so you can make several stitches at once. Allow a 1 cm (³/₈ in) space between the stitches. Use a long piece of thread, and when it runs out change colour, so that the colour changes are random.

4. Move the hoop around and repeat, filling the skirt with circles. Finish the threads by sewing them in at the back of the work.

X-STITCH

30

MATERIALS & EQUIPMENT

→ **Second-hand skirt, or about 2 m (2 yd) fabric for skirt base – use the pattern sheet provided**

→ Flower template E from pattern sheet

→ Heavy paper for stencil

→ Embroidery floss that is the same colour as the skirt but different in tone, plus a complementary colour

→ Blank screen

→ Printing foil and glue

→ Large embroidery hoop

SEE ALSO

Using an embroidery hoop, page 17
Freehand X-stitch, page 81
Transfer foiling, page 83

Here, instead of traditional cross-stitch the stitch is used as a mark-making tool, using the 'X' mark freehand, as if it were roughly drawn with a brush.

1. Cut out and make your skirt (see pages 8-27), or reclaim a skirt from a charity shop.

2. Attach the embroidery hoop to the skirt. Using the hoop as a guide, make crosses with a long needle. For every circle, make one cross that is in a complementary colour, so for example red and green, blue and orange, purple and yellow or black and white.

3. Fill the skirt with cross-stitched circles.

4. Lay the skirt out flat and using the flower stencil, screen and glue, apply foil flowers at intervals, overlapping the stitched circles. Allow to dry.

FLURO TAIL

31

MATERIALS & EQUIPMENT

→ **Second-hand skirt, or about 2 m (2 yd) fabric for skirt base – use the pattern sheet provided**
→ Tailor-tacking foot
→ Flower template E from pattern sheet
→ Heavy paper for stencil
→ Printing ink
→ Blank screen

SEE ALSO

Changing a foot, page 15
Tailor-tacking stitch, page 82
Making a stencil and using a silkscreen, page 83

This is made with a sewing machine foot, usually used in fashion, to do a tailor-tacking stitch – a loose stitch that is easy to pull out. It's good for making temporary marks, or really satisfying as a surface stitch that can be fluffy if cut, just like the surface of a long-pile carpet.

1. Cut out and make your skirt (see pages 8–27), or reclaim a skirt from a charity shop.

2. Using the straight edge of the skirt as a guide, draw a straight line using tailor's chalk, from the waistband to the hem. Make several more chalk lines parallel to the first, and about 2 cm (1 in) apart. These will be your guides.

3. Starting at the waistband of the skirt, sew using the tailor-tacking foot, for 10 lines minimum. Make more lines, around the skirt for as long as you like. Change the colour of the thread in the machine when it runs out to vary the lines.

4. Cut the stitches down the centre to create a fluffy texture. The stitches will now be loose, so iron fusible webbing to the reverse to secure.

5. Using the template and paper, make a stencil for your print. Lay your skirt out flat and using the paper stencil, print all over the stitches and remaining skirt base. Allow to dry, and then press on the reverse to fix the colour permanently.

PLOUGHED FIELDS

32

MATERIALS & EQUIPMENT

→ **Second-hand skirt, or about 2 m (2 yd) fabric for skirt base – use the pattern sheet provided**

→ Leftover fabric of the cut-out skirt base plus extra fabric

→ Circle template A and tractor J from pattern sheet

→ Heavy paper for stencil

→ Blank screen and printing inks

→ Transfer foil and foiling glue

→ Large brooch

SEE ALSO

Making a stencil and using a silkscreen, page 83

Transfer foiling, page 83

Making strips and pleating, pages 112–113

In Lisbon, Portugal, there is a shop that is seemingly devoted to deck chairs: replacement fabrics, narrow widths and beautiful, plentiful stripes. Surely, such delight is wasted on garden chairs?

1. Prepare your skirt and make a circle template, with a diameter of 40 cm (16 in). With the skirt on a flat surface, place the circle template 5 cm (2 in) up from the hemline and to one side. Draw around it using tailor's chalk.

2. Take your leftover and extra fabric and rip into 3 cm (1½ in) width strips. Choose fabric that has a close texture and colour relationship with the base fabric.

3. Sew the start of the first strip to the skirt, with the foot of your sewing machine on the left of the strip and on the line of your circle, so you are sewing in an anti-clockwise direction. Pleat the strip, as you are sewing onto the skirt – pinch 5 cm (2 in) of the fabric strip, and sew half way along the left-hand side of the pleat. Then pinch another 5 cm (2 in), and sew in a spiral,

until you get to the middle and have a blank circle about 5 cm (2 in) in diameter remaining. Finish the pleated circle with the large brooch.

4. Using tractor template J, make a paper stencil. Using the screen and stencil, print across the skirt, avoiding the ruffle, and leave to dry. Iron on the reverse to fix permanently.

5. Make the 40 cm (16 in) circle template used for the ruffle guidelines, into a paper stencil to print with. Using the foiling glue, print the circles all over the skirt (over the top of the first print). Print as many circles as you can fit onto the surface of the skirt, taking care again to avoid the ruffle, and apply the transfer foil.

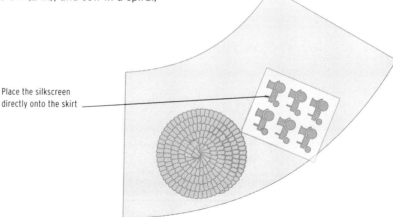

Place the silkscreen directly onto the skirt

BLANKETY BLANK

33

MATERIALS & EQUIPMENT

→ **Second-hand skirt with texture, or about 2 yd (2 m) brocade fabric for skirt base – use the pattern sheet provided**

→ Blank screen

→ Transfer foil and foiling glue

SEE ALSO

Making a lining, page 21
Transfer foiling, page 83

TIP

Textured fabric can be bought almost anywhere, and comes in a number of different patterns, the more defined the embossing in the fabric, the better for the print and finished product. The glue should be applied to the side of the fabric that is most prominent.

This skirt is made with a textured upholstery fabric, actually a pair of old curtains. Traditional Jacquard-woven brocade fabric has its pattern embossed naturally in its weave, and is a pleasure to work with. The foil shows up every detail of the pattern.

1. Cut out and make your skirt (see pages 8-27), or reclaim a skirt from a charity shop.

2. Take a blank screen and print the skirt with foiling glue all over. Once completely dry, apply the transfer foil following the instructions on page 83.

3. Make a contrasting coloured or patterned lining, and attach at the waistband.

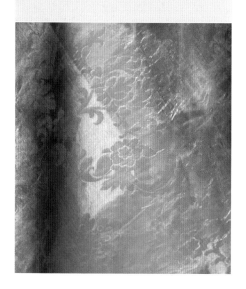

COCKEREL & PAPERCUT 34&35

MATERIALS & EQUIPMENT

→ **Second-hand skirt, or about 2 m (2 yd) fabric for skirt base – use the pattern sheet provided**
→ Blank screen and printing inks
→ Pack of papercuts
→ Heavy paper for template
→ Large or medium circle template A from pattern sheet
→ Assorted ribbon, braiding and Petersham tape
→ Brooches, buttons or beads

SEE ALSO
Making tags, page 31
Making a stencil and using a silkscreen, page 83

TIP
The papercut does gradually dissolve over time, and will wash straight off the screen in the end, but just keep printing and don't be put off by this – it's lovely to see a mark soften and disappear as it is being used.

Delicate tissue papercuts are a traditional folk craft in China and are available in some Chinese stores. You will need enough to fill your screen. They are so fragile they don't last being used as a screen stencil for long, so it may be best to buy several that are similar in design so that you can replace the ones that will disintegrate.

PAPERCUT

1. Cut out and make your skirt (see pages 8-27), or reclaim a skirt from a charity shop.

2. Measure the area of your blank screen and, on the corner of the skirt, roughly place down enough papercuts to fit the area of the screen.

3. Lay the screen over the top of the papercuts and print. The first print attaches the papercuts to the screen, so the prints thereafter are just a case of moving the screen and printing as quickly as possible, to get as much out of the papercuts as you can before they disintegrate.

Start in one corner and move the screen around to cover the whole skirt

4. When this is dry, place the large-or medium-sized circle template on the skirt so that it is to one side of the centre, and using tailor's chalk, draw around it.

5. Cut your ribbon, Petersham tape and braiding to 8 cm (3⅛ in) lengths. Fold these in half and sew them to the chalk line until they join up with the beginning of the circle. Measure 1 cm (³⁄₈ in) from the cut line of the ribbon and start the next circle of ribbon. Repeat until you have a circle of 30 cm (12 in) in diameter in the middle, and fill with brooches, buttons or beads.

COCKEREL

CUTTING & STICKING

Cutting and layering are techniques that lend themselves to decoration. Layers of paper and paint can be replicated in fabric to have the same effect. It is so satisfying seeing all those patterns, colours and different weights of fabrics, all in one finished garment − like the pages of a book.

The raw edge of a cut is decorative in itself, but some people may worry that it will fray and the item will fall apart. A skirt with raw edges all over can last for several years of hard wear − as long as the raw edge is not made out of a loose weave, you have nothing to worry about.

Fusible webbing is basically a double-sided adhesive that supports fabric and prevents fraying where you don't want it. Use it to create 'stickers' of patterned fabrics, one on top of another. To create a more intricate surface, sew or print on top as well.

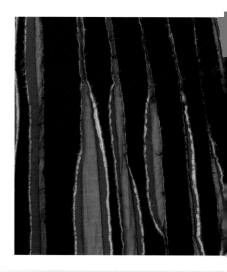

CUTTING THROUGH LAYERS
1 Place several layers of fabric together, using different colours, and as many tiers as you will be able to sew through. Make lines of stitching across the fabric, passing through all layers.

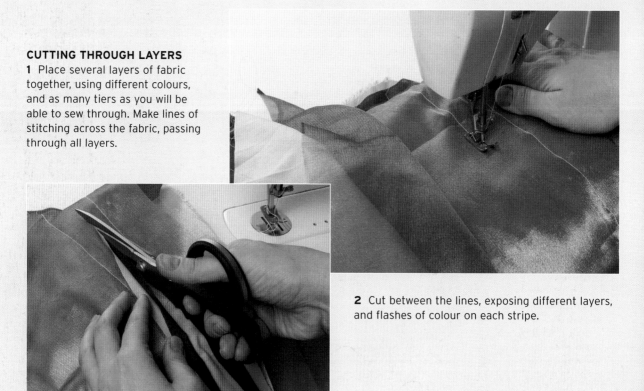

2 Cut between the lines, exposing different layers, and flashes of colour on each stripe.

USING FUSIBLE WEBBING

Appliqué is a decorative technique where a design is added to the surface of a fabric and stitched in place by hand, or machine. Traditionally, this was a slow process, but new products allow quick and easy results by fusing the design onto the fabric, rather than sewing.

1 Lay your paper-backed fusible webbing on top of your template or design, and trace the pattern. The pattern will be reversed, which is an important consideration if you are using type.

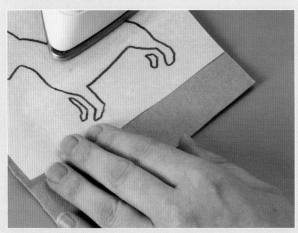

2 Iron the fusible webbing onto the wrong side of the fabric that is to be applied.

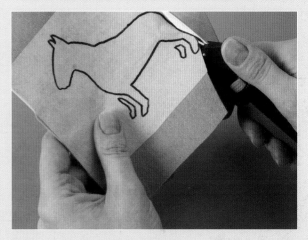

3 Cut around the design carefully.

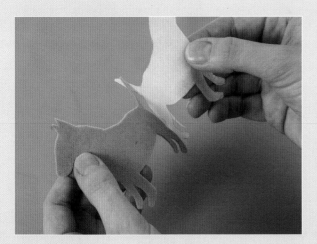

4 Remove the paper backing.

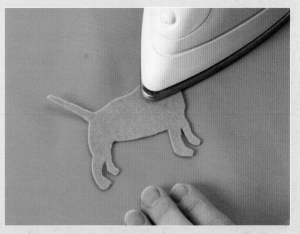

5 Place the design in its final position, and press into place with the iron. Allow to cool. To secure further, sew around the edge of the design with a running stitch, blanket stitch or a machine satin stitch.

BLACK RAINBOW & DOROTHY

36&37

MATERIALS & EQUIPMENT

→ **Second-hand skirt, or about 2 m (2 yd) fabric for skirt base – use the pattern sheet provided**

→ Large circle template A from pattern sheet

→ Heavy paper for template

→ 6-12 different-coloured or patterned lightweight fabrics, roughly 1 m (1 yd) squared

→ Dressmaker's pins

TIP

The fabrics must all be fine, for example, poplin or cotton lawn, so that all the layers are easy to sew through. The template doesn't have to be a circle; any geometric shape is possible.

SEE ALSO

Lady Cruella, page 106. Save all the circles that are cut out for use on another project.

Inspired by a sample book of fabric swatches, these skirts are a colourful, layered structure. Black on the outside, with a rainbow in the middle, Black Rainbow is composed of 12 layers, but remains wearable because of the lightweight fabrics used. Dorothy has half as many layers, and uses floral and geometric prints, just right for skipping down the yellow brick road.

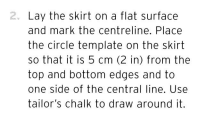

BLACK RAINBOW

1. Cut out and make your skirt (see pages 8-27), or reclaim a skirt from a charity shop.

2. Lay the skirt on a flat surface and mark the centreline. Place the circle template on the skirt so that it is 5 cm (2 in) from the top and bottom edges and to one side of the central line. Use tailor's chalk to draw around it.

3. Lay out the 10 fabrics on top of each other, in the order you want them to appear, and place under the chalk circle. Sew along the chalk line, so all eleven layers of fabric are joined together, in a smooth line – pin the fabric if you need to.

4. Measure 3 cm (1½ in) in from the sewn line, and cut around the circle, through one layer only, so you cut it out, and have the negative left. Repeat for every layer, cutting the next colour 3 cm (1½ in) from the last, and so on. When you have finished cutting the final layer, turn the skirt to the inside and trim all the square edges, following the sewn line, to end up with a smooth cut line.

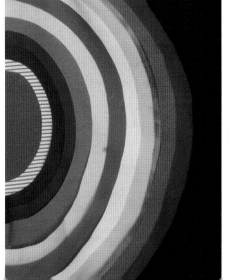

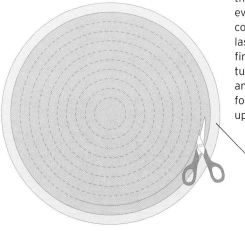

Starting at the outside edge of the circle, cut through one layer at a time

DOROTHY

THE OLD LADY WHO LIVED IN A SHOE

38

MATERIALS & EQUIPMENT

→ **Second-hand skirt, or about 2 m (2 yd) fabric for skirt base – use the pattern sheet provided**

→ Leftover fabrics

→ A shoe insole, or template H from pattern sheet

→ Heavy paper for template

SEE ALSO
Remaindered, pages 54-55

She had so many shoe-soles, she didn't know what to do, but I did. A shoe insole found in a second-hand shop was a beautiful geometric shape, and having lots and lots of fabrics leftover from former skirts inspired these multiples of the same shape using different fabrics of a similar tone.

1. Cut out and make your skirt (see pages 8-27), or reclaim a skirt from a charity shop.

2. Layer the leftovers one on top of the other. The pile should be as thick as you can make it, without distorting the fabrics when you cut out. Draw out one shoe insole on the top layer, and cut through all the layers. Make about thirty – you can do more if you need them.

3. Draw a line in tailor's chalk 2.5 cm (1 in) up from the hemline, all the way around the bottom of the skirt. Sew either end of the insole to the line, and roughly 2.5 cm (1 in) along the same line, sew another insole down. Repeat this until you have finished the line.

4. Make another chalk line 2.5 cm (1 in) up from the first line, and repeat until the whole skirt is full of insoles.

Note* Attach the lining before the last round is added.

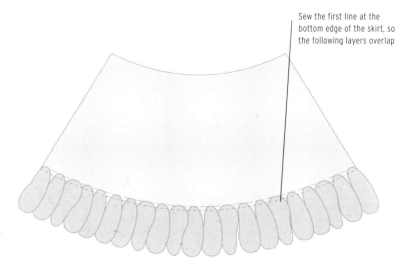

Sew the first line at the bottom edge of the skirt, so the following layers overlap

WILLESDEN'S FLOWERS

39

MATERIALS & EQUIPMENT

→ **Second-hand skirt, or about 2 m (2 yd) fabric for skirt base – use the pattern sheet provided**

→ Short length of doweling or broom handle

→ Floral fabric, with large flower print

→ Fusible webbing

→ Heavy paper for stencil

→ Blank screen and printing ink

SEE ALSO

Zigzag stitch, page 15
Making a stencil and using a silkscreen, page 83
Using fusible webbing, page 99

TIP

When choosing the patterned fabric to go with the skirt base, make sure the smallest amount of colour in the pattern is the same as the skirt base colour. This relates the two fabrics but not in an obvious way, and means that they 'match' without blending into each other. The larger the flowers, the easier they will be to cut out.

A mixture of polka dots, appliqué and screen-printing, this skirt uses fabric scraps as appliqué embellishment, and looks fabulous.

1. Cut out and make your skirt (see pages 8-27), or reclaim a skirt from a charity shop.

2. Lay out the skirt on a flat surface with a piece of paper to protect the rest of the skirt from the printing ink. Print the dots, using the doweling as a stamp. The spots can be close together or far apart. Do this freehand, so the design doesn't look too rigid. Spots can bleed off the edges of the skirt; this makes their placement look natural.

3. Take your patterned fabric and iron the fusible webbing to the reverse. Keep the paper on the webbing, as this makes it easier to cut out. Cut out the shapes, following the pattern of the fabric (florals are used here). Lay the skirt on a flat surface and arrange the floral shapes, either all over the skirt or clustered, and pin down. Remove the paper from the webbing, and iron onto the skirt. Sew either by hand or use a zigzag machine stitch around the shape's edges to secure them.

4. With a piece of paper the size of your silk screen, draw the outline of your fabric shape onto the centre of the paper, and cut it out so you are left with a paper stencil. Attach the stencil to the underside of the screen. Choose your printing colour and print the shape directly onto the skirt. In this example, the printed shape is the same size as the appliqué, so it doesn't overpower it.

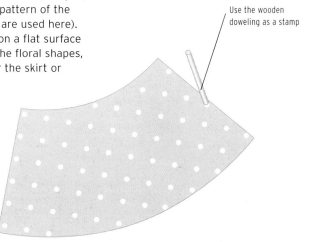

Use the wooden doweling as a stamp

LADY CRUELLA

40

MATERIALS & EQUIPMENT

→ **Second-hand skirt, or about 2 m (2 yd) fabric for skirt base – use the pattern sheet provided**

→ Rolls of both thin and wide white ribbon

→ Leftover fabric or circles from previous skirts

SEE ALSO
Cutting through layers, page 98

Inspired by a stripe fetish as well as a love of Audrey Hepburn in the racing scene in *My Fair Lady*, this skirt uses a bold black-and-white striped ribbon. The ribbon was found in a charity shop and makes an incredibly confident mark. The circles left over from making Dorothy and Black Rainbow (see pages 100–101) have been kept and sewn back onto this skirt.

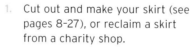

1. Cut out and make your skirt (see pages 8-27), or reclaim a skirt from a charity shop.

2. With a sewing machine, and following the straight edge of the skirt, sew all the ribbon flat, in strips, with a gap between each piece. Don't measure or mark the gaps, as the freehand variations will add to the charm. The ribbon will automatically move into a diagonal, just let it go in what direction it wants to.

3. When all the ribbon is sewn, place the circles on top of each other, so the largest is at the bottom and the smallest is at the top. Place this pile of circles on the skirt, so it is offset to one side.

4. Sew the pile onto the skirt by sewing in stripes 2 cm (³/₄ in) apart, all the way through the circles. Using sharp scissors, slice through the alley between each row of stitches, so all the fabrics underneath can be seen.

Sew vertical lines across the applied circles, then cut between them without cutting the base layer

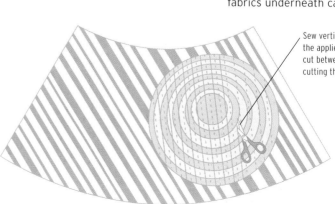

LACERATED STRIPES

41

MATERIALS & EQUIPMENT

→ **Fine fabric for skirt base, about 2 m (2 yd) in eight colours – use the pattern sheet provided**

SEE ALSO
Cutting through layers, pages 98

Striking black, red and turquoise are layered all the way through the construction of this skirt and not just on the surface.

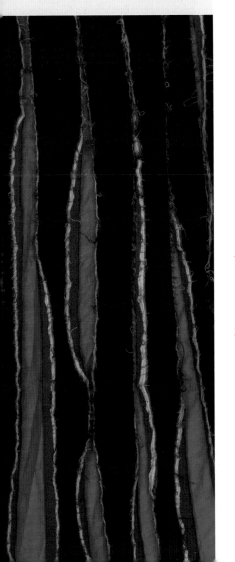

1. This skirt has 8 layers, so when cutting out your skirt (see pages 8-27), cut all the layers out at the same time.

2. Following the straight edge of the skirt, sew through the 8 layers of fabric and machine stitch lines with a 5 cm (2 in) gap between them. Using sharp scissors, slice through the alley between each row of stitches, leaving the base fabric, and the lining, free.

3. Using a hot iron, press the fabrics back so you can see all the layers sandwiched between the top and bottom layer of fabric.

PIECE OF CAKE

42

MATERIALS & EQUIPMENT

➜ **Second-hand skirt, or about 2 m (2 yd) fabric for skirt base – use the pattern sheet provided**

➜ Extra fabric from skirt base and a complementary fabric

➜ Circle template A from pattern sheet

➜ Heavy paper for template

SEE ALSO

Sewing fabric into seams, page 32

TIP

The extra seam will take 2 cm (³/₄ in) off the waistline of the skirt. Allow extra fabric, or ensure your old skirt will still fit. This technique is a great way to make skirts that are too large, fit again.

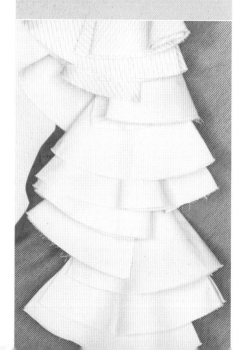

When cutting or ripping fabric, there are always beautiful bits left – it is a shame to throw these out. This surface is taken from an old-fashioned bustle, to be worn at the front or the back. Fabric circles are folded and sewn into a seam. It is actually very easy, and it makes you walk taller too.

1. Lay the skirt on a flat surface and find the centreline. Make a mark 10-12 cm (4-5 in) to one side with the tailor's chalk at the top and bottom edges. Using a measuring tape or yard stick as a guide, draw a line vertically down the centre of the skirt, cut the skirt in half, then fold the skirt so the right sides are facing.

2. Layer the extra fabrics one on top of the other, about 5 layers deep to save time. Using the circle template for discs as a guide, place it on the corner of your pile. Draw around it. You will now have an idea of spacing and can mark circles across the fabric. Cut out the circles.

3. Take a circle of fabric, and fold into a quarter circle. Starting at the waistband of the skirt, place the fabric onto the seam with the point on the edge of the cut line. Pin in place.

4. Add another quarter circle of fabric into the seam. Continue like this until you reach the hem. Tack the circles into place and remove the pins.

5. Place the other side of the skirt on top, right sides together, and sew along the seam with a 1 cm (³/₈ in) seam allowance. Backtack to secure the seam. Iron the seam flat, and trim the excess if the seam is bulky.

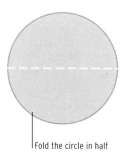

Fold the circle in half

In half again

And in half again

INVERTED RAINBOW

43

MATERIALS & EQUIPMENT

→ **Second-hand skirt, or about 2 m (2 yd) fabric for skirt base – use the pattern sheet provided**

→ Leftover fabric or circles from previous skirts

→ Circle template A from pattern sheet

→ Heavy paper for template

→ Colourful lining fabric

SEE ALSO
Frayed edges, page 26
Cutting through layers, page 98
Lady Cruella, page 106

TIP
Save all the offcuts from your sewing exploits, as you never know when they will be useful.

This skirt takes some of the leftover circles from previous skirts and, coupled with techniques from Lady Cruella and a brightly coloured lining, uses them to great effect.

1. Cut out and make your skirt (see pages 8-27), or reclaim a skirt from a charity shop.

2. Place the circles on top of each other, so the largest is at the bottom and the smallest is at the top. Place this pile of circles on the skirt, so it is offset to one side. If you don't have leftover circles, you can cut some more using the circle template A.

3. Sew the pile onto the skirt by sewing in stripes 2 cm ($^3/_4$ in) apart, all the way through the circles. Using sharp scissors, slice through the alley between each row of stitches, so all the fabrics underneath can be seen.

4. Wash the skirt so that the fabric frays and the colours merge. Allow the edges of the cuts to fray. If some pieces of fabric hang free, this will just add to the overall effect.

5. Add a colourful lining that is slightly longer than the main skirt to finish.

RUFFLES & RUCHING

Ruffles are layers of fabric in a concentration of pattern and colour. Ruffles are present everywhere; frilly knickers, petticoats, rosettes, a man's dress shirt, the middle of roses ....

You may not have enough gorgeous fabric for a whole skirt, but it is always enough for a ruffle. If you are sent, given or recycling fabric, you may not have the choice of lengths of cloth, but here you have a technique that will enable elaborate creations from any piece of fabric, whatever its dimensions.

It is possible to use a special machine that ruffles fabric, or a sewing machine foot that performs the same task. But ruffling by hand is straightforward and quick.

TIP
If you are using a second-hand skirt as your base, choose fabric for your strips that has a close texture, and colour relationship, to the existing material. Use the selvedge of fabrics, as it is usually a different colour, or may have type on it, which adds interest.

MAKING STRIPS
Rip or cut strips of fabric along the straight grain, to the width indicated in your pattern – between 3-6 cm (1$\frac{1}{2}$-2 $\frac{1}{4}$ in) – and as long as the fabric allows. Make a snip with sharp scissors, and then tear along the grain to make a straight line.

Once you have a pile of ripped strips, take your first strip and remove any excess threads. Iron the strip so it is perfectly flat, and place to one side. Repeat this for all of the strips.

These long strips will be used to pleat, or ruche, following either a straight chalk line or a chalk circle.

PLEATING

1 Lay your base fabric out flat. To pleat the strip, pinch 5 cm (2 in) of fabric and fold under, then pin. Then pinch another 5 cm (2 in) and pin. Keep going until the strip runs out. To join a new strip, place the short end of fabric under the last pleat, and continue as before.

2 Using a sewing machine, or by hand, straight stitch along the left-hand side of the pleat. If the pins are placed across the line of stitching, it avoids the need to baste. However, be sure not to hit a pin, as the needle may break and have to be replaced. Pin the next line of pleating so that it overlaps this sewn line.

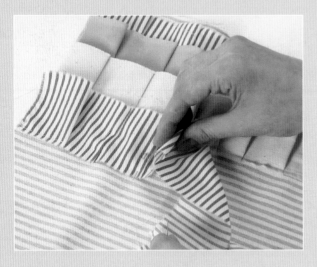

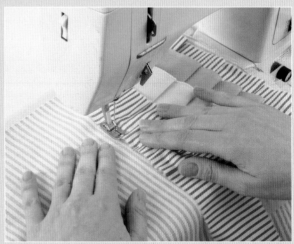

RUCHING

1 Following the chalk line for your design, sew along the top, or left, side of the strip. As you are sewing, push the fabric through toward the foot and under the needle, so that the strip ruches slightly and is gathered under the line of stitching, while keeping the base fabric flat.

2 When starting a new strip, conceal the raw end under the gathers of the previous strip. Make the next line of ruching above this one, so that the lines of stitching are neatly concealed.

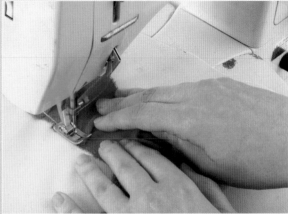

DENIM RUBY

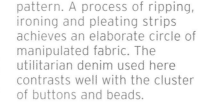

MATERIALS & EQUIPMENT

→ **Second-hand skirt, or about 2 m (2 yd) fabric for skirt base – use the pattern sheet provided**

→ Circle template A from pattern sheet

→ Heavy paper for template

→ Leftover fabric from the skirt base, plus an extra 1 m (1 yd) of fabric

→ Brooches, buttons or beads

SEE ALSO
Using a paper pattern, page 18
Using found objects, page 60
Making strips, page 112
Pleating, page 113

TIP
When sewing the middle of the ruffle with the brooches, buttons or beads, try and make it as elaborate and encrusted as possible. A small area with so much detail will sparkle beautifully with the frayed denim.

This technique uses the fabric that is leftover after cutting-out a pattern. A process of ripping, ironing and pleating strips achieves an elaborate circle of manipulated fabric. The utilitarian denim used here contrasts well with the cluster of buttons and beads.

1. Cut out and make your skirt (see pages 8-27), or reclaim a skirt from a charity shop.

2. Make a circle template from paper, so that the diameter measures 10 cm (4 in) less than the length of your skirt. Lay the skirt on a flat surface and mark the centreline. Place the circle template on the skirt so that it is 5 cm (2 in) from the top and bottom edges, and to one side of the central line. Use tailor's chalk to draw around it.

3. Take your leftover and extra fabric and rip into 3 cm (1½ in) width strips.

4. Sew the start of the first strip onto the chalk line of your circle, with the foot of your sewing machine on the left of the strip, so that you are sewing in an anti-clockwise direction. Pleat the strips as you go along. To pleat the strip, pinch 5 cm (2 in) of the fabric and pleat as you are sewing onto the skirt. Sew half way along the left-hand side of the pleat and then pinch another 5 cm (2 in) and sew.

5. Sew in a spiral, until you get to the middle and have a blank circle of about 30 cm (12 in) in diameter remaining. Finish the pleating and fill the middle with all the brooches, buttons and beads, sewing them on by hand.

ONION'S RUFFLE

45

MATERIALS & EQUIPMENT

→ **Second-hand skirt, or about 2 m (2 yd) fabric for skirt base – use the pattern sheet provided**

→ Dog template B from pattern sheet

→ Heavy paper for stencil

→ Leftover fabric from the skirt base plus about 1 m (1 yd) extra fabric

→ Large brooch or button

→ Silkscreen and printing ink

SEE ALSO
Making a stencil and using a silkscreen, page 83

Dogs are lovely, but living in a city, it can be difficult to keep one, so fulfill your desire for a dog by making a skirt decorated in them. This skirt contains several techniques blended together: printing, stencilling and ruffling. The ruffle is a small embellishment on the right or left of the skirt.

1. Cut out and make your skirt following steps 1-3 for Denim Ruby on page 114.

2. Add pleats using the same technique as used in step 4 of Denim Ruby. Sew the pleats in a spiral, until you get to the middle and have a smaller blank circle of about 5 cm (2 in) in diameter remaining. Fill the middle with maybe one dramatic brooch, one large button or multiples of both.

3. Create a paper stencil the same size as your screen by copying the dog template B on the pattern sheet and repeating

it at intervals. With the paper stencil and a blank printing screen, print across the skirt and the spiral with the printing ink. Leave to dry and then iron on the reverse to fix, or follow the manufacturer's instructions.

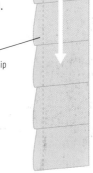

Sew over the folds of the strip when pleating

AMBIDEXTROUS CHIFFON

46

MATERIALS & EQUIPMENT

→ **Second-hand skirt, or about 2 m (2 yd) heavyweight fabric for skirt base – use the pattern sheet provided**

→ Chiffon in 6 different colours, either silk or polyester, approximately 6 m (6½ yd)

SEE ALSO
Ruching, page 113

TIP
To support layers of chiffon, the base fabric needs to be quite heavy, for instance, denim, canvas or cotton twill.

Chiffon is beautifully fine and fluid but, for the same reason, sewing it can be really tricky. Because the chiffon is translucent, plenty of strips layered together achieve a surface that is almost like mixing paint, effectively changing the colour of a fabric without dyeing it.

1. Cut out and make your skirt (see pages 8-27), or reclaim a skirt from a charity shop.

2. Rip or cut the chiffon into strips 6 cm (2¼ in) wide.

3. Using tailor's chalk, draw a horizontal line 2 cm (¾ in) up from the hemline, all the way around the bottom of the skirt.

4. When you have done this, put 6 different-coloured chiffon strips together, one on top of another, and following the line, sew them down, pushing the strips toward the needle, so that it ruches under the line of stitches.

5. Make another line about 2 cm (¾ in) above this row and make another row of ruching. Repeat this process all the way to the top of the skirt.

6. The top layers of chiffon strips will cover up all the stitching that is underneath. Make the lining last, and take the top edge of the ruching inside the waistline seam.

RAW RUFFLE

47

MATERIALS & EQUIPMENT

→ **Second-hand skirt, or about 2 m (2 yd) fabric for skirt base – use the pattern sheet provided**

→ Leftover fabrics that complement the skirt base

→ Petersham tape or ribbon, 1¼ m (4 yd)

SEE ALSO

Making a lining, page 21
Making strips, page 112
Pleating, page 113

This is a ruffled skirt that will work as well on its own, or under any skirt as a petticoat. Here it is shown under a plain foiled skirt. Use up all those scraps and leftovers, from linings as well as the skirt base.

1. Cut out and make your skirt (see pages 8–27), or use a reclaimed skirt from a charity shop. If you are using a second-hand skirt, choose fabric that has a close texture and colour relationship with the base fabric.

2. Take your leftover fabric and rip into 3 cm (1½ in) width strips.

3. Draw a line in tailor's chalk 1 cm (³⁄₈ in) up from the hemline, all the way around the bottom of the skirt. Sew the start of the first strip onto the chalk line.

4. To pleat the strip as you sew, pinch 5 cm (2 in) of the fabric strip and sew half way along the left-hand side of the pleat. Then pinch another 5 cm (2 in) and sew. Once you have finished the line, sew exactly the same on the reverse of this ruffle, so that the petticoat is double-sided.

5. Depending on how much surface you want to cover with ruffles, use 3 lines of ruffles on each side. Move up the skirt, and when you have finished ruffling, sew a piece of ribbon or Petersham tape to the top of the ruffle to hide the raw edge.

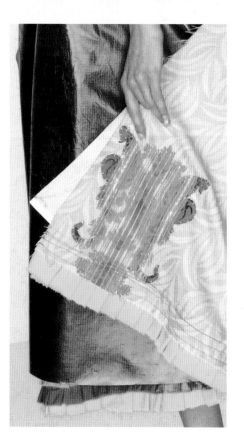

RAINBOW

MATERIALS & EQUIPMENT

→ **Second-hand skirt, or about 2 m (2 yd) fabric for skirt base – use the pattern sheet provided**

→ Oval template D from pattern sheet

→ Heavy paper for stencil

→ Leftover and scrap fabrics – any colour, weight or pattern

→ Leather scraps

→ Leather punch and white glue

SEE ALSO
Using found objects, pages 60-61
Making strips, page 112
Pleating, page 113

As its name suggests, this skirt uses the colours of the rainbow, and then some. Every inch of the skirt is covered with ovals of pleating. Make each line of pleats a different shade.

1. Cut out and make your skirt (see pages 8-27), or reclaim a skirt from a charity shop.

2. Make an oval template, roughly measuring 60 cm (23½ in) long and 34 cm (13⅓ in) wide. Lay the skirt on a flat surface. Using the template and tailor's chalk, draw ovals onto the skirt so they are flush with each other, in any composition you like.

3. Take your leftover or extra fabric and make 3 cm (1½ in) width strips. Take the first strip, and in an anti-clockwise direction, sew 1 cm (⅜ in) of the strip on the left side, onto the drawn line, to secure the strip to the skirt. To pleat the strip, pinch 5 cm (2 in) of fabric, and sew half way along the left-hand side of the pleat. Then pinch another 5 cm (2 in) and sew. Keep sewing until you have a gap approximately 3 cm (1½ in) wide in the middle.

4. Punch circles or strips out of the leather and attach to the centre of the oval with white glue.

5. Sew on the leather decorations until the skirt is full, filling in the gaps between the ovals.

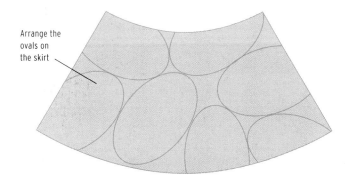

Arrange the ovals on the skirt

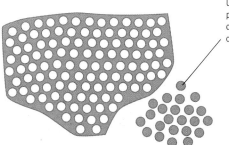

Use a leather punch to make circles in different colours of leather

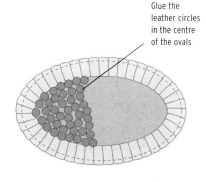

Glue the leather circles in the centre of the ovals

SPRUNG

49

MATERIALS & EQUIPMENT

→ **Second-hand skirt, or about 2 m (2 yd) fabric for skirt base – use the pattern sheet provided**
→ Heavy paper for stencil
→ Circle template A and flower template E from pattern sheet
→ Off-cuts of fabrics that complement the skirt base
→ Artificial flowers
→ Silkscreen
→ Transfer foil and glue
→ Glue gun

SEE ALSO
Using plastics, page 61
Making a stencil and transfer foiling, page 83
Making strips and pleating, pages 112-113

The ruffles on this bright rosette are broader than before, to create a dramatic three-dimensional decoration.
Use shades of one colour, or contrasting colours for a vibrant effect.

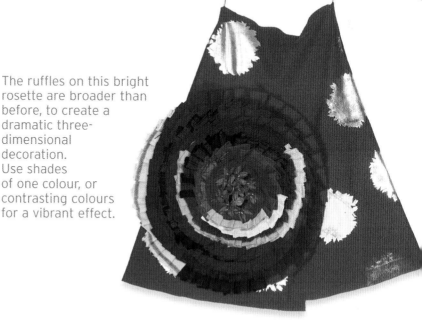

1. Cut out and make your skirt (see pages 8-27), or use a second-hand skirt.

2. Make a stencil from the flower template, and print with foiling glue. Attach the foil and iron to fix in place.

3. Lay the skirt on a flat surface and mark the centreline. Place the circle template on the skirt so that it is to one side of the central line. Use tailor's chalk to draw around it.

4. Using your leftover or extra fabric, create 6 cm (2¼ in) width strips (see page 31). Sew the start of the first strip onto the line of your circle, with the foot and needle of your sewing machine on the left of the strip, so you are sewing in an anti-clockwise direction.

5. To pleat the strip, as you are sewing onto the skirt pinch 5 cm (2 in) of the fabric, and sew half way along the left-hand side of the pleat. Then pinch another 5 cm (2 in), continuing around the circle (see page 113).

6. Sew in a spiral, until you get to the middle and have a blank circle of about 5 cm (2 in) in diameter left. Fill the middle by attaching artificial flowers with the glue gun (see page 61).

1ST PRIZE

49½

MATERIALS & EQUIPMENT

→ **Second-hand skirt, or 1.5 m (1½ yd) fabric for skirt base – use the pattern sheet provided**

→ Circle template A from pattern sheet

→ Paper for template

→ Leftover fabric of the cut out skirt base and extra fabric

→ Large brooch, button or beads

This is a short skirt, with a big ruffle. Market research into different-sized women shows that even though the ruffle is large in proportion to the skirt base, both short and tall women can wear this skirt and look great.

1. Cut out and make your skirt (see pages 8-27), or reclaim a skirt from a charity shop. This skirt is shorter, knee-length instead of calf-length. Measure from your natural waistline to your knee to get your personal measurement, and shorten your pattern (see page 18).

2. Using template A, make a circle with the paper so that the diameter (approximately 50 cm/ 20 in) almost fills one side of the skirt. Lay the skirt on a flat surface and mark the centreline. Place the circle template on the skirt so that it is 5 cm (2 in) from the top and bottom edges and to one side of the central line. Use tailor's chalk to draw around it.

3. With the leftover fabric, make the strips, and following the chalk line, pleat the strip, as you sew – pinch 5 cm (2 in) of the fabric, and sew half way along the left-hand side of the pleat. Then pinch another 5 cm (2 in), continuing around the circle (see page 113).

4. Continue to sew and pleat in a spiral until you get to the middle, and have a blank circle of about 5 cm (2 in) in diameter remaining. Fill the middle with maybe one brooch, one large button or multiples of both.

GLOSSARY OF TERMS

APPLIQUÉ
This is a decorative technique where a design is added to the surface of a fabric and stitched in place by hand or machine. Traditionally this was a slow process, but new products allow quick and easy results by fusing the design onto the fabric rather than basting into place.

BACKTACKING
Sewing back and forth at the start and end of a row of machine stitching to secure the threads.

BROCADE
Brocade is a crisp, bulky fabric with a surface design woven on a Jacquard loom. The design is created by raised surface threads that give a pattern on both sides of the cloth.

FABRIC
The result of yarns having been woven or knitted together. In some cases, fibres are felted or bonded directly into fabric.

FIBRE
A single natural or synthetic 'hair', which is then spun with others into a yarn.

FUSIBLE WEBBING
This is a paper-backed fusible adhesive that irons on, adhering on both sides.

GRAIN
Woven fabric is made up of warp and weft threads. In plain weaves these are at right angles to each other. Tearing will only go along the grain, so will create a straight line in natural fibres.

JACQUARD
A type of loom that creates textured designs through operating the threads of the warp independently.

PETERSHAM TAPE
This is a specially made tape, similar in appearance to grosgrain ribbon. The scalloped edge allows the tape to bend easily around corners. This tape is traditionally used to make waistbands stiff.

SEAM ALLOWANCE
The distance between the stitching line and the edge of the fabric when sewing pieces together. A standard 1-1.5 cm ($3/4$-$5/8$ in) is often used, depending on the confidence of the sewer. Decide how much allowance you need before cutting your fabric.

SELVEDGE
The finished edges of a woven cloth that do not unravel.

SHEARS
Long-bladed scissors for cutting through fabric.

SILKSCREEN
This is a wooden or metal frame with a fine mesh fabric stretched over one side. Ready-made screens are widely available, or you can make one with undyed silk chiffon stapled to a wooden stretcher. Specialist mesh can be bought commercially, and should have about 80 to 100 threads per inch.

SILKSCREEN INKS
These are made to a particular consistency so that they fit through the mesh of the screen without bleeding. Mix inks with a special fabric binder that can be permanently fixed to the fabric with the application of heat (follow the manufacturer's instructions).

SQUARE KNOT
The square knot or reef knot, is a common and simple binding knot. To tie a square knot, pass right over left, then left over right.

TOP AND EDGE STITCHING
These are rows of decorative stitching visible on the surface of fabric to define the structure of a garment and to reinforce areas.

Top stitching is often worked close to the edge of seams; edge stitching is sewn right on the border to emphasise it and create a crisper finish. Use top stitching and edge stitching together or individually.

TRANSFER FOIL
This is commercially available metallic foil that adheres to fabric with heat or pressure. Follow the manufacturer's instructions.

TWILL WEAVE
A weave with an obvious diagonal rib on the surface.

WAFFLE WEAVE
A decorative woven fabric that is difficult to tear.

WARP
This refers to the threads put on the loom first before a fabric is woven. The weft threads are then woven between them.

WEFT
The threads making up the filling yarns of a woven cloth.

RESOURCES

Petersham tape, ribbon, buttons and fabric scraps can be found all over the place. Try your local charity shops, and flea markets, but above all, recycle what you already have.

SUPPLIERS

Quality Colours – foil glue, binder and inks
Unit 13, Gemini Project,
Landmann Way,
London SE14 5RL
Tel: +44 (0)207 394 8775

London Screen Services – silkscreens
Unit 75,
Parkside Business Estate,
Blackhorse Road,
London SE8 5H2
Tel: +44 (0)208 6949 717

R. A. Smart – foil
R. A. Smart, Clough Bank,
Grimshaw Lane, Bollington,
Macclesfield,
Cheshire SK10 5NZ,
Tel: +44 (0)1625 576231
www.rasmart.co.uk/

Baynham And Stanfield Badge Company Limited – bulk badges
32b Coppice Trading Estate,
Stourport Road,
Kidderminster, DY11 7QY
Tel: +44 (0)1562 60738
www.baynhambadges.co.uk

Kleins – online store for braid, buckles and fastenings
5 Noel Street
London W1F 8GD
Tel: +44 (0)20 7437 6162
www.kleins.co.uk

The Bead Shop
20 Beak Street
London W1F 9RE
Tel: 020 7629 9964
www.creativebeadcraft.co.uk

MacCulloch & Wallis – unusual fabric store with millinery department
25–26 Dering Street
London W1S 1AT
Tel: +44 (0)20 7629 0311
www.macculloch-wallis.co.uk/

WEBSITES

www.sewingpatterns.com
Patterns from the most popular pattern companies on sale online

www.isew.co.uk
Hints and tips, and news of events

www.sewing.org
Non-profit organisation aiming to get people sewing

besewstylish.taunton.com
Online resource and sew blogs

www.madeirausa.com
Information about threads and stabilisers and where to buy them

INDEX

CREDITS

With special thanks to:

Borovick Fabrics Limited

16 Berwick Street
London
W1F 0HP

www.borovickfabricsltd.co.uk